Creating Adaptive Policies

Creating Adaptive Policies

A GUIDE FOR POLICY-MAKING IN AN UNCERTAIN WORLD

Edited by
Darren Swanson
Suruchi Bhadwal

International Development Research Centre
Ottawa • Cairo • Dakar • Montevideo • Nairobi • New Delhi • Singapore

 www.sagepublications.com
Los Angeles • London • New Delhi • Singapore • Washington DC

First published in 2009 by

SAGE Publications India Pvt Ltd
B1/I-1 Mohan Cooperative Industrial Area
Mathura Road, New Delhi 110 044, India
www.sagepub.in

SAGE Publications Inc
2455 Teller Road
Thousand Oaks, California 91320, USA

SAGE Publications Ltd
1 Oliver's Yard
55 City Road
London EC1Y 1SP, United Kingdom

SAGE Publications Asia-Pacific Pte Ltd
33 Pekin Street
#02-01 Far East Square
Singapore 048763

**International Development
Research Centre**
P.O. Box 8500
Ottawa, ON
Canada K1G 3H9
www.idrc.ca
info@idrc.ca
ISBN (e-book) 978-1-55250-467-3

Published by Vivek Mehra for SAGE Publications India Pvt Ltd, typeset in 10/12 pt Arno Pro by Star Compugraphics Private Limited, Delhi and printed at Chaman Enterprises, New Delhi.

Library of Congress Cataloging-in-Publication Data

Creating adaptive policies: a guide for policy-making in an uncertain world/edited by Darren Swanson and Suruchi Bhadwal.
    p. cm.
  Includes bibliographical references and index.
    1. Sustainable development—Government policy. 2. Environmental policy. 3. Adaptive natural resource management. 4. Policy sciences. I. Swanson, Darren. II. Bhadwal, Suruchi.

HC79.E5C7275   320.6—dc22   2009   2009025081

ISBN: 978-81-321-0147-5 (HB)

The SAGE Team: Rekha Natarajan, Manali Das, Rajib Chatterjee and Trinankur Banerjee

Contents

List of Tables and Figures

TABLES

FIGURES

Foreword

The imperative to marry our pursuits of economic, social and environmental well-being has never been so urgent. At the same time, the setting in which policy-makers must work has never been so complex and uncertain. And now the backdrop to this increasing urgency is a worsening global economic crisis, the likes of which most of us have never experienced—a crisis that came as a surprise to the majority of policy-makers.

We are in danger of approaching a perfect storm of global crises. A global food crisis reared its head early in 2008 and has not gone away, and the impacts of climate change are manifesting themselves faster than was projected some years ago as carbon continues to accumulate in our atmosphere at unprecedented rates. But with these unfortunate experiences we are learning some important lessons about our economy, society and environment. For example, the economic crisis illustrates just how interconnected our local and global economies have become. The food crisis has reminded us of the vulnerability of the poor to fluctuations in market prices for our most fundamental commodities. The climate change issue has illustrated the interconnections among our economy, our society and our environment. The carbon fuelling our economy is changing the global environment on a scale never experienced before.

It is indeed a very complex, dynamic and uncertain world.

This is the stage on which policy-makers try to improve the lot of their citizens. Our respective organizations—the International Institute for Sustainable Development (IISD) and The Energy and Resources Institute (TERI)—strive to help governments incorporate the principles of sustainability into decision-making. Among these principles are: that we understand and appreciate the inherent interconnectedness of the pressing economic, social and environmental issues; that those who have much should be accountable to those who have little; and that we, as the present generation, are accountable to the next generation of citizens who have no voice in today's decisions.

Advancing public policies and business decisions that put these principles into action is the mark of a mature society. Doing so is a daunting task even under the best and most stable of conditions. But today's conditions are far from stable. Putting these principles into practice, when the operating environment of a policy is highly dynamic, unpredictable and uncertain—as is the reality for most of today's pressing issues—is extremely difficult. An unprepared policy in such a setting has a good chance of not achieving its objective or having unintended negative consequences, or both. Such policies become a hindrance to advancing quality of life and sustainability.

Creating Adaptive Policies was written to help policy-makers navigate today's complex, dynamic and uncertain terrain—to help policies help people. The authors began with an extensive search of the literature. What at first sounded like solos on how to deal with such complex policy settings from disparate sectors—including business, transportation engineering, healthcare, natural resources and Internet communications, to name a few—became a symphony when the lessons learned from across this range of economic sectors were all heard together. A common thread in these lessons was an appreciation of the policy environment as a complex adaptive system, a conceptual understanding that illuminated many important characteristics of how people interact among themselves and with their environment. The authors then listened to the people on the ground most impacted by public policies, including farmers and water resource managers in Canada and India. Policies that helped these persons deal with the dynamics and uncertainty of fluctuations in weather exhibited many of the adaptive features that were observed in the literature.

Contained in the chapters of this book are seven tools that have helped policy-makers design and implement policies that perform in highly dynamic and uncertain settings. Adaptive policies anticipate the array of conditions that lie ahead through robust design using: (1) integrated and forward-looking analysis, including scenario planning; (2) multi-stakeholder deliberation to illuminate potential pitfalls and unintended consequences and (3) by monitoring key performance indicators to trigger automatic policy adjustments.

But not all situations can be anticipated in advance through diligent use of analytical and deliberative tools. Adaptive policies are also able to navigate towards successful outcomes in settings that cannot be anticipated in advance. The book describes how this can be done by working in concert with certain characteristics of complex adaptive systems, including: (1) enabling self-organizing and social networking in communities (2) decentralizing decision-making to the lowest, and most effective and accountable unit of governance; (3) promoting variation in policy responses; and through (4) regular and systematic policy review and improvement—always examining whether assumptions about intended outcomes are accurate.

As introduced in Chapter 1, these seven tools are being applied by policy-makers and managers in many economic sectors to deal with a variety of policy issues. If you are a policy-maker working on the climate change issue you will find this book useful for crafting policies to tackle both mitigation and adaptation. If you are dealing with agriculture or water resource management issues, you will relate to many of the case examples presented in the book. Regardless of the arena of public policy and governance for which you have responsibility, we are confident that this book will be a welcome addition to your toolbox.

David Runnalls
Rajendra K. Pachauri

Acknowledgements

The International Institute for Sustainable Development (IISD) and The Energy and Resources Institute (TERI) appreciate the generous support of Canada's International Development Research Centre (IDRC).

We would also like to acknowledge the Climate Change and Impacts Branch, Natural Resources Canada, for its financial support of IISD's Prairie Climate Resilience Project, the field work from which several of the Canadian policy case studies were identified for this book. Field work undertaken in Canada by graduate students Peter Myers and Kent Pearce, under the supervision of Fikret Berkes at the University of Manitoba's Natural Resources Institute, was instrumental in helping to identify policies from which adaptive features could be examined.

We are grateful for the early intellectual contributions of Preety Bhandari and Ulka Kelkar from TERI in India, and to the sage advice and keen interest of Simon Carter and Marco Rondon of IDRC. The advice and review provided by TERI's executive director, Leena Srivastava, in the later stages of the project is also greatly appreciated.

We would also like to thank the following individuals from government, academia, and the private and non-profit sectors for their input during the course of the project:

A.S. Dhingra, Aditi Kapoor, Ajaya Dixit, Andrew McCoy, Anil Gupta, Anne Hammill, Blair McClinton, Brad Williams, Brett Dotter, Bryan Oborne, Candace Vanin, Cathy Hummelt, Christa Rust, Conference of the Parties—United Nations Framework Convention on Climate Change, Dale Rothman, Dave Sauchyn, David Radcliffe, Debbie Nielson, Dennis Haak, Doug McKell, Djordjija Petkoski, Drew Perry, Ed Dean, Elain Fox, Fikret Berkes, Guy Lafond, Harry Daiz, Institute for Public Administration of Canada, International Conference on Adaptive & Integrated Water Management, Jack Ruitenbeek, Jennifer Medlock, Jim Hiley, Jo-Ellen Perry, John Vandal, K.C. Momin, Ken Meter, Ken Schykulski, Kent Pearce, Liz Fajber, Lorna Hendrickson, Louise Smith, Lyn Gallagher, Malcolm Black, Marcus Moench, Neil Cunningham, Niranjan Pant, Oliver Puginier, Paul James, Paul Vincent, Pavan Kumar Singh, Peter Myers, Prodipto Ghosh, Richard Margoluis, R.R.B.R. Thabbah,

Sangeet Srivastava, Scott Stothers, Seema Bhatt, Shashikant Chopde, Sholom Glouberman, S.K. Barik, S.K. Dalal, Stephen McGurk, Subodh Sharma, Sunil Augustine, Surya Sethi, T.S. Panwar, Teresa Raines, Terry Zdan, Vincent Marchau, Vivek Kumar, Warren Walker, Wayne Gosslin, Wayne Hjertas and William H. Glanville.

Finally, on behalf of all the authors, we thank our families for their love and understanding during our time spent away from home in preparation of this book.

Darren Swanson
Suruchi Bhadwal

1 The Need for Adaptive Policies

Henry David Venema and John Drexhage

THE CHALLENGE FACING POLICY-MAKERS

Today's policy-maker has a tough job. Crafting public policies to help guide the daily actions of individuals, communities and businesses to ensure our economic, social and environmental well-being, is challenging under the best of circumstances. But the reality is that our world is more complex than ever—highly interconnected, owing to advances in communication and transportation; and highly dynamic, owing to the scale of impact of our collective actions. We know, for example, that the climate is changing, but not precisely how. We know that energy prices are highly unpredictable, and that international trade rules are in a state of flux. Advancing human well-being through policy, therefore, is inherently complex and dynamic. Whether policies seek to address economic conditions such as household income levels; social issues such as infant mortality rates; or environmental matters such as availability of clean water, today's policy- and decision-makers face significant uncertainty.

Policies that cannot perform effectively under dynamic and uncertain conditions run the risk of not achieving their intended purpose, and becoming a hindrance to the ability of individuals, communities and businesses to cope with—and adapt to—change. Far from serving the public good, these policies may actually get in the way. Experience demonstrates that policies crafted to operate within a certain range of conditions are often faced with unexpected challenges outside of that range. The result is that many policies have unintended impacts and do not accomplish their goals. Therefore, policy-makers need ways to craft policies that can adapt to a range of conditions previously not imagined and can perform even under complex, dynamic and uncertain conditions.

This book provides practical guidance for making adaptive policies— policies that can anticipate and respond to an array of conditions that lie ahead, and can navigate towards successful outcomes when surprised by the unforeseen.

In preparing this book we first undertook a comprehensive review of academic and professional insights on how to intervene effectively in complex adaptive systems as experienced by a range of sectors including natural resources management, healthcare, transportation engineering, information technology and international development. To study more closely the adaptive features of public policies, we examined and researched case examples from agriculture and water resources management within a context of weather uncertainty and all of the socio-economic and ecological issues enveloped in the global climate change issue. From hundreds of interviews with farmers and water resource managers in Canada and India we identified policies that have helped people and communities adapt to historic weather-related shocks and stresses. We did so based on the belief that such policies would be fruitful ground for researching specific adaptive policy-making mechanisms. And this indeed turned out to be the case. From over a dozen policy examples that we studied in Canada and India, we unearthed many specific and practical features that policy-makers have employed to make policies adaptive. We draw from these examples throughout the book (and summarize them at the back) to illuminate seven things we observed that policy-makers should know to create better policies in today's complex, dynamic and uncertain world. We tested our ideas at numerous workshops and international meetings and prepared this book as a guide for adaptive policy-making relevant for socio-ecological settings and the pursuit of sustainable development.

THE IMPERATIVE: SUSTAINABLE DEVELOPMENT AND THE PROSPECTIVE MIND

We are motivated in this work by the imperative for a sustainable future, a future in which decisions are made with careful, deliberative thought about positive and negative impacts as viewed from economic, social and environmental perspectives, and with due regard for present and future generations. Fundamental to this pursuit is the ability of people to interact with each other and adapt to change. Public policies have an important role to play in fostering this ability. But for policies to be effective and to help people, the policies themselves must also give careful consideration to complex interactions and be able to adapt to conditions that can and cannot be anticipated. A policy that is unable to continue to perform in a dynamic and uncertain setting, or unable to detect when it is no longer relevant, is a policy that is more likely to hinder the freedom and capability of people to adapt to change.

Some of the leading intellectual lights of our era are coming to terms with perhaps the fundamental challenge of human development. In his 2008 book, *Common Wealth: Economics for a Crowded Planet*, eminent American economist Jeffrey Sachs argues passionately that out of sheer necessity the logic and wisdom of sustainable development—the simultaneous and inter-related pursuit of social, environmental and economic objectives—will take centre stage. Along the way—again out of sheer necessity—we will overturn deeply-seated, but evermore anachronistic notions about governance.

Sachs' diagnosis is blunt: 'the current trajectory of human activity is not sustainable' (2008: 57). Our collective appropriation and abuse of the Earth's natural resources, particularly the productivity of its ecosystems, is well beyond sustainable levels—as is our abuse of resources not substitutable such as clean air, clean water and food.

The world food security crisis experienced in 2008 places these issues in sharp relief. Global food prices rose by 83 per cent between 2005 and 2008. The United Kingdom think tank, Chatham House, argues that although the food crisis is viewed as a demand-side issue, namely a lack of purchasing power in some food-insecure countries, it is in fact symptomatic of multiple-scarcity pressures on the supply side, primarily energy scarcity, unsustainable land-use pressure, diversion of food crops for biofuels and the key impact of climate change—water scarcity. The global financial crisis which reared its head in 2008 is yet another example of the complex interconnections that have emerged in society and the degree of surprise and uncertainty that confronts today's policy-maker.

Responding to the fundamentally co-mingled challenges of climate change, energy scarcity and food security will be the defining challenge for this gen-eration of policy-makers—whose kitbag of policy approaches, according to Sachs, needs substantial upgrading.

Political scientist and best-selling author Thomas Homer-Dixon recently articulated for policy-makers what he refers to as *the upside of down* (Homer-Dixon, 2006). The downside is the inevitable catastrophic surprises that have shocked and devastated societies, both present and past. The upside is that we are learning from past failures and are beginning, albeit ever so slowly, to change our conventional way of thinking of the world as a predictable machine, to using our mental capacities for self-criticism and reflection—to better see the signals that can alert us when things are going wrong and in need of course correction. This improved understanding and appreciation of the inherently complex, dynamic and uncertain nature of socio-economic and ecological systems he calls the prospective mind. A policy-maker with a prospective mind knows that the only thing we do know about the future is that surprise, instability and extraordinary change will be regular features of our lives. A policy-maker with a prospective mind, as Homer-Dixon describes, seeks to make our societies more resilient to external shock and more supple in response to rapid change.

SIGNS OF ADAPTIVE POLICY-MAKING

This book can be thought of as a guide to cultivating the prospective mind— capable of embracing the inherent complexity and uncertainty of real-world policy-making. The guidance in this book emerges from the recent experiences of policy-makers and the insights of academics and practitioners for dealing with complex adaptive systems and pursuing adaptive policies and management.

Signs of the imperative for adaptive policy-making are coming from all sectors of our economy including healthcare, transportation, business, information technology, energy, international development, agriculture and natural resources management, to name but a few. We highlight these examples in the following sections and believe this is clear evidence that a transition in public policy-making is underway, from traditional approaches which assume the future is knowable and manageable using static policies, to a more adaptive approach that understands and appreciates dynamics, uncertainty and the complexity of socio-economic and ecological interactions.

Climate Change Mitigation Policy

> *Apply GHG emission reduction policies that incorporate adaptive management practices and have built-in monitoring and assessment mechanisms to allow for regular reviews to ensure efficiency and effectiveness.*
>
> Canada's National Round Table on the
> Environment and the Economy (2007)

In 2007 Canada's National Round Table on the Environment and the Economy published a report entitled *Getting to 2050: Canada's Transition to a Low-emission Future* (NRTEE, 2007). There was a formal request by the Government of Canada to study climate change and air pollution policies and to provide advice on how Canada could significantly reduce its greenhouse gas and air pollutant emissions by 2050. The report prepared by the Round Table explored the economic and environmental implications associated with a low-emission future and assessed potential policies to reach long-term commitments.

The report's recommendations demonstrate that, 'with consideration for some key enabling conditions and acknowledgement of certain risks and uncertainties, this transition is manageable, and may even provide some unique opportunities' (NRTEE, 2007). One of the five recommendations related to greenhouse gas emissions reductions was to 'apply GHG emission reduction policies that incorporate adaptive management practices and have built-in monitoring and assessment mechanisms to allow for regular reviews to ensure efficiency and effectiveness'. The recommendation goes on to note that following such an adaptive approach will 'ensure that progress is monitored, compliance issues are addressed, and policies are adjusted to match the required level of abatement effort, and will minimize and mitigate unanticipated adverse outcomes'.

Water Resources Management

When situations are characterized by variability, uncertainty and change, conventional planning scenarios provide little guidance regarding future needs and conditions.

Moench et al. (2003)
Water Resources Management in India

A group of water resource managers and researchers working in India and Nepal set out to capture lessons learned from local water management issues involving disputes between proponents of large dams or inter-basin transfers and advocates of local approaches to meeting water requirements (Moench et al., 2003). Their context was that water resources in the region face a dual challenge of scarcity and pollution, which 'not only threaten the resource base but also undermine the foundation of society and community livelihood'. Their research revealed that although it might be possible to identify some emerging issues with conventional approaches, it is the case that 'changing conditions often render specifically targeted management proposals irrelevant or impossible to implement' (ibid.: 9). The authors concluded that there is a 'clear need for frameworks that are adaptive—which reflect uncertainties and can respond as contexts change or unforeseen problems emerge' (ibid.).

Noteworthy from the perspective of understanding the need for adaptive policy approaches is their conclusion that 'specific solutions are less important than the existence of processes and frameworks that enable solutions to be identified and implemented as specific constraints and contexts change' (ibid.). For example, their research in the Tinau watershed in Nepal found that adaptive responses to water management should 'be able to both reflect local contexts and adapt as conditions change' (ibid.: 16). Furthermore, their research in the Sabarmati Basin in India highlights the advantages of using models as a communication tool and the need for engaging all stakeholders to find solutions for complex water management issues.

Agriculture

> ... *if climatic uncertainty and variability are on the rise due to climate change ... we must shed our blinkered equilibrium views and solutions and search for alternatives that allow for living with uncertainty.*
>
> Scoones (2004)
> Pastoral Rangeland Management in Africa

In 2004 Ian Scoones wrote that much can be learned from the pastoral rangelands of the world, where uncertainty has always been a part of everyday life and survival. He describes these as regions 'where systems are not at equilibrium, where sometimes chaotic, often stochastic, dynamics prevail and where predictability and control are false hopes' (Scoones, 2004). His observation from working in many parts of Africa was that the assumptions for rangeland ecology in these regions were 'fundamentally flawed' and resulted in 'wildly inappropriate' solutions. Scoones concluded that if climatic uncertainty and variability are on the rise due to climate change, then 'we must shed our blinkered equilibrium views and solutions and search for alternatives that allow for living with uncertainty'.

He contends that conventional views of institutions as static, rules-based, formal, fixed and having clear boundaries are giving way to views that institutions must be dynamic, overlapping, heterogeneous, socially defined, emergent from adaptive practice and flexible. He warns that if we do not change our way of intervening in these settings, we may soon find ourselves in a state of non-equilibrium where our own policies and underlying assumptions may soon become 'wildly inappropriate'.

Healthcare

> *Cities are enormously complex and changes in one part of the city may produce unforeseen consequences in another. Human health is a product of many factors, each of which interacts with others, and each of which is subject to change that may affect the overall health of an individual.*
>
> Glouberman et al. (2003)
> Health in Cities

A group of healthcare researchers and practitioners in Canada set out to find a better policy approach to improving health in cities (Glouberman et al., 2003). The *Urban Health* approach focused on 'identifying and understanding vulnerable communities ... or particular diseases or syndromes that are of concern primarily in cities'. The *Healthy Cities* approach recognizes 'the importance of interactions between individual and the natural, built, and social environment'. The researchers found that, unfortunately, neither approach had been adequate because cities and health are very complex and unpredictable: 'the parts of the system interact and change in the face of shifting circumstances, and this change often occurs in ways that could not be deducted from the characteristics of the individual elements in isolation'. The reality, they recognize, is that communities and groups often compete for limited money and services, so policy interventions directed at certain groups 'may inadvertently lead to reduced attention to other communities' (Glouberman et al., 2003).

The approach that was eventually crafted captured the important features of both the urban health and healthy cities approaches, but had a stronger theoretical basis for intervention. They needed 'an approach that recognized both the particular vulnerabilities and problems faced by specific populations within the urban environment, but also addressed the effects of the urban environment on all city residents'. Previous approaches focused almost exclusively on the 'problems', whereas the strengths and assets of the population had been largely invisible and not leveraged to address health issues.

Grounding their approach in complex adaptive systems theory, Glouberman et al. (2003) proposed a toolbox for improving health in cities. Among the recommendations were that policy interventions should promote variation because 'introducing small-scale interventions for the same problem offers greater hope of finding effective solutions'. This is based on the understanding that 'many interventions will fail and that such failures are simply a feature of how one develops successful interventions in complex adaptive systems' (ibid.). They also understood that possible solutions undergo selection by the system; therefore, it is important to include 'evaluating performance of potential solutions, and selecting the best candidates for further support and development' (ibid.).

Energy

In the 1970s, despite the price of oil having been stable for some time, a few planners at Royal Dutch Shell were concerned about factors that might affect the price. Most notably, a new organization was emerging that could potentially have enough clout to impact the global price of oil, that being OPEC—the Organization of Petroleum Exporting Countries. The Shell planners started to develop stories about the future that described the full ramifications of sudden changes in oil prices—stories that made senior executives 'feel the shocks'

(Schwartz, 1991). Two plausible futures were articulated: one about a future with stable oil prices; the other about a future of sharply increasing oil prices as influenced by OPEC and other factors (ibid.).

The innovative scenario planning efforts of Royal Dutch Shell paid off. The anticipated oil price shock indeed came a few years later, and of the large oil companies of the day, only Shell was prepared for it. From among the weakest of seven companies, Shell gained a unique source of competitive advantage by re-perceiving the future (not predicting it) and became one of the two most profitable companies of that day. This scenario planning process helped managers at Shell to 'clarify their assumptions, discover internal contradictions in those assumptions, and think through new strategies based on new assumptions' (Senge, 1990).

To this day Shell continues its scenario planning activities, and perhaps by no coincidence, remains a top company in its field.

Transportation

> *Public policies must be devised in spite of profound uncertainties about the future.*
> *When there are many plausible scenarios of the future, it may well be impossible to*
> *construct any single static policy that will perform well in all of them.*
>
> Walker and Marchau (2003)
> Civil Aviation and Airport Expansion

A group of transportation researchers and planners in the Netherlands were motivated to find a better way to address uncertainty in socio-technical systems (Walker and Marchau, 2003). They used the expansion of Schiphol Airport in Amsterdam to illustrate the problems with the classical policy-making approach and the benefits of a new adaptive policy approach. The issue with the Schiphol Airport was one of capacity to accommodate growth in the future in light of growth in the number of passengers, noise issues, the amount of cargo transported and other issues. It was acknowledged that 'a design approach that combines an assessment of the costs and benefits of a variety of infrastructure options, with uncertain assumptions about future demand provides a shaky foundation for the specification of a policy for civil aviation in the Netherlands for the next 30–40 years' (RAND Europe, 1997).

As a better approach to this issue, they suggest that policies be 'adaptive— devised not to be optimal for a best estimate future, but robust across a range of futures'. Their notion of adaptive policies includes policies 'that respond to changes over time and that make explicit provision for learning'. This approach requires that learning and adaptation of the policy be made 'explicit at the outset' and the inevitable 'policy changes become part of a larger, recognized process and are not forced to be made repeatedly on an ad hoc basis' (Walker and Marchau, 2003). For example, they recommend monitoring signposts (for example, profitability of the anchor airline) that can trigger certain contingency plans, such as attracting other hub airlines to the airport.

Information Technology

Although complexity is often perceived as a liability, it can be harnessed. So, rather than seeking to eliminate complexity, we explore how the dynamism of a complex adaptive system can be used for productive ends.

Axelrod and Cohen (2000)
Internet Information Technolgy

The information technology sector published a seminal piece in 2000 called *Harnessing Complexity: Organizational Implications of a Scientific Frontier* (Axelrod and Cohen, 2000). Funded by the US Department of Defense, this research project constructed a theoretical framework of complex adaptive systems with the purpose of understanding how the theory could be harnessed for policy related to the Internet information technology wave.

The researchers found that conditions that favoured variation, interaction and selection (picking and choosing what seems to work best in certain situations), fostered successful outcomes. They cite the example of the Linux computer operating system. This system has become a highly reliable not-for-profit software package—the result of contributions from thousands of unpaid programmers that is competing with for-profit operating systems developed and sold by Microsoft, Sun and IBM (ibid.).

International Development

... there is no evolution or progress without interactions; members of the population have to be free and able to interact for anything to happen.

Rihani (2002)
International Development

Rihani (2002) takes a critical view of international development efforts over the past several decades and observes that 'at base, development is what nations do as complex adaptive systems, and what they do can be described as uncertain evolution that has no beginning or end, nor shortcuts, and few signposts on the way'. His conclusion is that 'rigid plans and policies are inappropriate' and that the only feasible approach for nations is 'to exercise flexibility and pragmatism in order to survive, learn and adapt over and over again'. But progress will not occur without interactions, and he further concludes that 'members of the population have to be free and able to interact for anything to happen'.

As noted earlier, Jeffrey Sachs also warns that solutions to 21st century's problems will be complex. 'The problems of sustainable development inevitably cut across several areas of professional expertise, making it hard for any single ministry—or academic department, for that matter—to address the issues adequately' (Sachs, 2008). Addressing African poverty will require strategies that 'simultaneously tackle disease control, agricultural modernization, ecological conservation, fertility control, the upgrading of infrastructure, and a host of other components'. He further reminds us of the interconnectedness of international development issues by describing that a 'sound climate change strategy must be informed by climate science, environmental engineering, energy systems, economics, ecology, hydrology, agronomics, infectious disease control, business, and finance'.

THE STRUCTURE OF THIS GUIDEBOOK

This book is the culmination of four years of research undertaken by the International Institute for Sustainable Development (IISD) based in Canada and The Energy and Resources Institute (TERI) in India. Financial support and advice for this initiative was provided by Canada's International Development Research Centre (IDRC).

Motivated by the pursuit for sustainable development, we present in this book seven tools that policy-makers can use in order to craft more adaptive policies in today's complex, dynamic and uncertain world. As two non-governmental organizations, IISD and TERI have over 50 years of collective operational experience in sustainable development research and practice. We have observed closely the critical need for policy-making approaches that match the complexity of sustainable development.

This guidebook is structured as follows:

- In Chapter 2 we introduce the seven tools, giving an initial grounding in the policy design and implementation cycle.
- Chapters 3 through 9 describe each of the seven adaptive policy tools individually. Each of these chapters are organized in a similar manner, providing (1) the rationale for why the adaptive policy tool is important; (2) a description of what the tool is; (3) a discussion of how the tool

could be used, (4) when in the policy-making cycle the tool can be used and, finally (5) relationships to the other adaptive policy tools discussed in the book. A summary table describing these elements is provided at the end of each chapter.

- The book concludes with Chapter 10 providing insights into implementing adaptive policies.

The specific case examples drawn on throughout the book may resonate most closely with policy-makers working in agriculture and water resource management sectors, and for policy-makers dealing with climate change issues, because that is the context from which the cases were drawn. But the seven tools for creating adaptive policies are relevant to any complex policy issue, providing a means to craft and implement policies under dynamic and unpredictable socio-economic and ecologic circumstances. We are confident that you will find the guidance provided in the chapters to follow a welcomed addition to your policy toolbox.

2 Seven Guidelines for Policy-making in an Uncertain World

Darren Swanson, Stephan Barg, Stephen Tyler, Henry David
Venema, Sanjay Tomar, Suruchi Bhadwal, Sreeja Nair,
Dimple Roy and John Drexhage

THE EMERGENCE OF ADAPTIVE POLICY CONCEPTS

Some of the first discussion about adaptive policy-making actually emerged in the early 1900s. Dewey (1927, in Busenberg, 2001) put forth an argument proposing that 'policies be treated as experiments, with the aim of promoting continual learning and adaptation in response to experience over time'. In 1978, Canadian ecologist C.S. Holling introduced natural resource managers to the notion of adaptive environmental assessment and management and paved the way for future thinking with regard to adaptive policies in socio-ecological settings.

In 1993 the term 'adaptive policy' appears in the published literature in Kai Lee's book that integrated science and politics for the environment—as experienced in the highly contested issue of salmon fisheries restoration and hydropower development in the Pacific Northwest of the United States. Taking a socio-ecological perspective, Lee described adaptive policy as *designed from the outset to test clearly formulated hypotheses about the behaviour of an ecosystem being changed by human use*' (Lee, 1993). Around the same time Dennis Rondinelli recommended that international development efforts be reorientated to '*cope more effectively with inevitable uncertainty and complexity of the development process*' (Rondinelli, 1993). He contends that one of the most promising ways to achieve this reorientation is to use '*an adaptive approach that relies on strategic planning, on administrative procedures that facilitate innovation, responsiveness and experimentation, and on decision-making processes that join learning with action*'.

In a special issue of *Integrated Assessment* in 2003, Warren Walker and Vincent Marchau from the Delft University of Technology in the Netherlands introduced a socio-technical perspective of adaptive policies and policy-making, and took the concept to a more pragmatic level. Motivated by the uncertainties surrounding policies relating to transportation safety and design they suggest that policies be '*adaptive—devised not to be optimal for a best estimate future, but robust across a range of futures*'. Their notion of adaptive policies includes policies *that respond to changes over time and that make explicit provision for learning*. This approach requires that learning and adaptation of the policy be made *explicit at the outset* and the inevitable *policy changes become part of a larger, recognized process and are not forced to be made repeatedly on an ad hoc basis* (Walker and Marchau, 2003).

The US National Academy of Science provides some additional practical insight into adaptive policies. Bankes (2002) recognized that '*most policy problems involve complex and adaptive systems and that for those problems, the classical approaches of predictive modeling and optimization that have been used in decision support software are not appropriate*'. He contends that for policies to be successful in a complex and adaptive world, policies will '*need to be adaptive themselves*', and warns that relying on optimization techniques to develop policies based on the projections of a single model will produce static policies which make the 'correct move' only for the best estimate model.

Holling's elucidation of adaptive management in 1978 is particularly noteworthy. Adaptive management can be described as learning by judicious doing. It is characterized by its flexible policies and the plurality of views that inform it; no particular epistemic community can possess all the necessary knowledge to form policy. Science, models, expert knowledge and the policies based on them are not interpreted as ultimate answers, but merely as a means to guide a cautious process of intervention in complex ecosystems. The goal of management shifts from achieving a single target to an integrated view of maintaining ecosystem resilience, avoiding, for example, catastrophic and irreversible 'flips' to other equilibrium states (Holling, 2001).

For a general definition of 'policy', 'policy instruments' and a description of an idealized policy design and implementation cycle, see Box 2.1.

Box 2.1   What is Policy?

A discussion of adaptive policies must first begin by establishing some common vocabulary. A *policy* can be thought of as a broad statement of purpose and process for addressing a particular social, economic or environmental issue. The intent of a policy is implemented via *policy instruments* such as regulatory (for example, laws and regulations); economic (for example, taxes, subsidies); expenditure (for example, research and development, education and awareness, targeted projects and programmes); and institutional instruments (for example, sector strategies).

(Box 2.1 Continued)

(*Box 2.1 Continued*)

The policy cycle consists of two main parts:

- **Design**—defining the rules for how the policy instrument is to perform and
- **Implementation**—the actions of the people and organizations that implement the rules of the policy instrument.

These two components are illustrated in Figure 2.1 which presents an idealized process of policy design and implementation. Policies are designed with varying degrees of consultation with relevant stakeholders and it is typically the case that an institution or organization different from the one which designed the policy is responsible for implementing the policy.

Consider, for example, a law for automobile speed limits. Penalties for drivers who exceed the speed limit are defined by government policy and law-makers. The policy is implemented by a police officer that stops the speeding driver. The police officer then has discretion on how to implement the policy. Depending on the actual speed of the driver and the road conditions at the time, the officer will decide on a warning or issue a speeding ticket. The police department may decide that speeding is an issue that will be given either low or high enforcement priority.

Figure 2.1   Idealized Illustration of Policy Design and Implementation

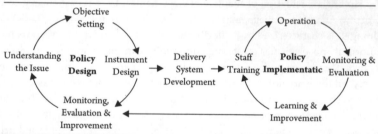

Policy design and implementation is an iterative cycle. Ideally it starts with understanding the issue as the precursor to setting the objective(s) of the policy. The necessary policy instrument(s) is then designed and an implementation process developed. This ideally starts with staff training to allow operation of the policy instrument. Implementation is monitored and periodically evaluated to learn what works well and what does not, and important improvements are made. Feedback from on-the-ground implementation on whether policy objectives are being met should make its way back to policy designers to better understand the issues and make critical improvements in the design, as well as, the implementation of the policy.

WHAT ARE ADAPTIVE POLICIES?

A brief history of the emergence of adaptive policies illustrates that this is not an entirely new concept. And in our field and desk research of policies in Canada and India, we observed many examples of policies that exhibit one or more features that have made the policy adaptive in some manner. But to reiterate the message from Chapter 1, we are living in a much more complex and dynamic world today; therefore, the need for adaptive policy-making approaches is now more urgent than ever. The time is right to take stock of the insights and lessons learned from existing and past policies, and the available academic literature, and provide policy-makers with a focused set of tools for policy-making in complex, dynamic and uncertain settings. We have spent four years researching this very task. This chapter offers our interpretation and compilation of what an adaptive policy is and what specific tools can be used to make policies adaptive.

Adaptive policies are designed to function more effectively under complex, dynamic and uncertain conditions. Adaptive policies anticipate the array of conditions that lie ahead through robust up-front design using (1) *integrated and forward-looking analysis*; (2) *multi-stakeholder deliberation* and (3) by monitoring key performance indicators to trigger *automatic policy adjustments*. But not all situations can be anticipated. Unknown unknowns will always be part of policy-making. Adaptive policies are able to navigate towards successful outcomes in settings that cannot be anticipated in advance. This can be done by working in concert with certain characteristics of complex adaptive systems, including (1) *enabling the self-organization and social networking capacity of communities*; (2) *decentralizing governance to the lowest and most effective jurisdictional level*; (3) *promoting variation in policy responses* and (4) *formal policy review and continuous learning.*

Designers and implementers of adaptive policies embrace the uncertainty and complexity of policy context, and consider learning, continuous improvement and adaptation of the policy a natural part of the policy life-cycle.

The adaptive policy approach we describe in this book is framed by the need for policy to have the capacity to adapt to both *anticipated* and *unanticipated* conditions—those conditions under which the policy must be implemented. It is understood that if policy-makers put enough effort into understanding the context of the issued being addressed, and enough analytic effort into understanding cause–effect relationships, we can anticipate much about how the policy will perform in the future and prepare the policy accordingly.

And policy-makers strive for such preparation, but there is still considerable room for improvement in the policy design and implementation process to build into policies the ability to adapt to anticipated conditions.

Building the capacity of a policy to adapt to unanticipated conditions is newer territory for policy-making. A policy-maker who believes that the future is inherently impossible to predict with accuracy, is ready to work with the approaches and tools that are presented in this book. In our experience in working with policy-makers and their advisors, this represents the vast majority.

The challenge facing policy-makers is that the world is a much different place than the one in which previous generations of policy-makers worked. The connectedness of the global economy, the pace of change and scale of impact of our actions, all add up to a more complex, dynamic and uncertain setting in which policy-makers must work on a day-to-day basis. New policy approaches and tools are needed to work effectively in this world. The good news is that many adaptive features have been employed in a range of existing policies and a growing number of policy-makers and academics are recognizing the need for these tools. The authors of this book believe the time is right to take stock of these new approaches, study them further and make them readily available to policy-makers.

PRINCIPLES FOR ADAPTIVE POLICIES

In Chapter 1, we illustrated that many sectors of our economy are pursuing more sophisticated policy design and implementation approaches based on an understanding and appreciation of a new and higher degree of interconnectedness and dynamic consequences. The vast majority of these pursuits ground their recommendations for policy intervention in the theory or concepts of complex adaptive systems. There is a large and growing literature on this, and valuable insights can be gleaned towards identifying a set of principles to help guide adaptive policies and policy-making for socio-ecological systems.

Perhaps one of the most lucid descriptions of a complex adaptive system was provided by Glouberman et al. (2003) while searching for ways to improve health in cities. They described a complex adaptive system as being...

> ...made up of many individual, *self-organizing elements* capable of responding to others and to their environment. The entire system can be seen as a *network*

of relationships and interactions, in which the whole is very much more than the sum of the parts. *A change in any part of the system,* even in a single element, *produces reactions and changes in associated elements and* the environment. Therefore, the effects of any one intervention in the *system cannot be predicted with complete accuracy,* because the *system is always responding and adapting* to changes and the actions of individuals. (emphasis added)

Most policy practitioners will identify with this as a reasonable depiction of the policy setting in which they work. Unpredictability and the presence of unknown unknowns are the underlying traits. This complexity comes from the adaptive nature of people (and the economy they create), combined with the adaptive nature of ecosystems. Both need to be analyzed and understood to the greatest degree possible to define the basket of policy input factors and potential outcomes that can be *anticipated,* but with some recognition that the system can never be understood or predicted with complete accuracy. The conundrum is that the contents of the basket of unanticipated factors and outcomes will never be clear. Certainly what at one point in time was not anticipated becomes anticipated through additional analysis, and experimental and experiential learning. But the unknown unknowns will always be lurking around the corner. So analytical and deliberative efforts focused on anticipating are necessary for adaptive policy-making, but they are not sufficient. It is how a policy can be designed and implemented in order to provide people and ecosystems with the best opportunity possible to deal adequately with the unknown—this is what makes a policy truly adaptive.

Rihani (2002) proposed that 'at base, development is what nations do as complex adaptive systems, and what they do can be described as uncertain evolution that has no beginning or end, nor shortcuts, and few signposts on the way'. We subscribe to the idea that the interaction of humans and nature through socio-economic processes are complex adaptive systems.

For over a decade, leading thinkers in the business sector have promoted a systems perspective to identify solutions for complex management problems. For example, Peter Senge based his best-selling theory of organizational learning on systems thinking, which he described as the discipline for seeing the structures that underlie complex situations and the best leverage points for change—it is the antidote for the sense of helplessness that everyone feels in this new age of interdependence. He goes on to describe that systems thinking offers a language that begins by restructuring how we think (Senge, 1990).

The recent study and application of complex adaptive systems can be seen in numerous fields including business management, healthcare, information technology, transportation, sustainable development and international development. Within these fields, practitioners and researchers have been thinking about how to better craft policies that can be effective in highly complex, dynamic and uncertain settings. Many of the examples cited in Chapter 1 base their insights either directly or indirectly on complex adaptive systems. Table 2.1 summarizes these insights, which are elaborated upon in

Table 2.1   Principles for Intervention in Complex Adaptive Systems

Stage of the Policy Cycle	*Principles for Intervention in Complex Adaptive Systems*
Policy set-up Understanding the issue and policy objective setting	• Respect history (Glouberman et al., 2003)
	• Understand local conditions, strengths and assets (Glouberman et al., 2003)
	• Understand interactions with the natural, built and social environment (Glouberman et al., 2003; Holling, 1978)
	• Look for linkages in unusual places (Ruitenbeek and Cartier, 2001)
	• Determine significant connections rather than measure everything (Holling, 1978)
	• Public discourse and open deliberation are important elements of social learning and policy adaptation (Steinemann and Norton, 2003)
	• Build trust, collaboration, consensus, identity, values, hope and capacity for social action (Forester, 1999)
	• Use epistemic communities to inform policy design and implementation (Haas, 1992)
Policy design and implementation	• Create opportunity for self-organization and build networks of reciprocal interaction (Axelrod and Cohen, 2000; Berkes et al., 2003; Glouberman et al., 2003)
	• Ensure that social capital remains intact (Ruitenbeek and Cartier, 2001)
	• Promote effective neighbourhoods of adaptive cooperation (Axelrod and Cohen, 2000)
	• Members of the population have to be free and able to interact (Rihani, 2002)
	• Facilitate copying of successes (Axelrod and Cohen, 2000; Ruitenbeek and Cartier, 2001)
	• Clear identification of the appropriate spatial and temporal scale is vital to integrated management (the ecosystem ap-proach; UNEP, 2000)
	• Match scales of ecosystems and governance and build cross-scale governance mechanisms (Berkes et al., 2003)
	• Promote variation and redundancy (Berkes et al., 2003; Holling, 1978)
	• Encourage variation (Axelrod and Cohen, 2000; Glouberman et al., 2003)
	• Balance exploitation of existing ideas and strategies and exploration of new ideas (Axelrod and Cohen, 2000)

(Table 2.1 Continued)

(Table 2.1 Continued)

Stage of the Policy Cycle	Principles for Intervention in Complex Adaptive Systems
Monitoring and continuous learning and improvement	• Integral to design are the monitoring and remedial mechanisms—should not be post *ad hoc* additions after implementation (Holling, 1978)
	• Fine-tune the process (Glouberman et al., 2003)
	• Learning and adaptation of the policy be made explicit at the outset and the inevitable policy changes become part of a larger, recognized process and are not forced to be made repeatedly on an *ad hoc* basis (Walker and Marchau, 2003)
	• Policies should test clearly formulated hypotheses about the behaviour of an ecosystem being changed by human use (Lee, 1993)
	• Learn to live with change and uncertainty (Berkes et al., 2003)
	• Policies should be expected to evolve in their implementation (Majone and Wildavsky, 1978; Sabatier and Jenkins-Smith, 1999)
	• Increase information on unknown or partially unknown social, economic and environmental effects (Holling, 1978)
	• Conduct selection (Glouberman et al., 2003)
	• Understand carefully the attribution of credit (Axelrod and Cohen, 2000)

Chapters 3 through 9. These insights can be thought of as a set of principles for how to intervene in complex adaptive systems.

For example, as already noted in Chapter 1, it has been proposed in the transportation sector that public policies be '*adaptive—devised not to be optimal for a best estimate future, but robust across a range of futures*' and that policies '*respond to changes over time and make explicit provision for learning*' (Walker and Marchau, 2003).

In the healthcare field, it is recommended that policy interventions should *promote variation* because '*introducing small-scale interventions for the same problem offers greater hope of finding effective solutions*'. This is based on the understanding that 'many interventions will fail and that such *failures are simply a feature of how one develops successful interventions* in complex adaptive systems' (Glouberman et al., 2003). It is also understood that *possible solutions undergo selection* by the system. It is therefore important to include '*evaluating performance of potential solutions, and selecting the best candidates for further support and development*' (ibid.).

In the forestry management sector, it is suggested that foremost for intervention in complex adaptive systems, policies must *ensure that social capital remains intact*—if local groups and their networks are disempowered individually or collectively, existing social structures are in effect invalidated and undermined (Ruitenbeek and Cartier, 2001).

In the natural resources management field it is understood that to build resilience in communities for complexity and change, interventions should promote self-organization by building networks of reciprocal interaction, matching scales of ecosystems and governance, and promoting variation and redundancy in actions (Berkes et al., 2003).

SEVEN THINGS POLICY-MAKERS SHOULD KNOW TO CRAFT ADAPTIVE POLICIES FOR TODAY'S DYNAMIC AND UNCERTAIN WORLD

We have learned through this past century that policy-making is certainly not mechanistic. The 19th century American poet John Godfrey Saxe, likened laws (policy) to sausages—it is best not to see them being made! As we navigate progress in the 21st century, we must learn to see policy-making as adaptive—more like gardening[1]: muddy, attentive and experiential, because we really do not know what growing conditions will prevail.

Our understanding of adaptive policies is framed by two types of capacities: (1) the capacity of a policy to adapt to anticipated conditions and (2) the capacity to adapt to unanticipated conditions. The capacity to adapt to *anticipated* conditions is founded in an understanding and appreciation of cause-and-effect and outcomes. This is the more traditional of the two capacities, although, that said, it is by no means a well-formed ability in most policy-making processes. A policy with this capacity can be crafted to:

- perform well under a range of anticipated conditions with little or no alteration;
- monitor changes in context and identify when these are significant enough to affect performance and
- automatically trigger timely policy adjustments *or* deliberations necessary to determine policy adjustments to maintain performance or terminate the policy when it is no longer relevant.

The capacity of a policy to adapt to *unanticipated* conditions is a much newer notion. Herein lays a new focus for policy-making. It is based on a holistic appreciation of system complexity, capacity, performance and dynamics. The boundary between what is anticipated and unanticipated does change.

---

[1] Based on conversations with Sholom Glouberman. Baycrest Medical Centre, Montreal, Quebec, Canada.

What was unknown one day (the unanticipated), might well be known the next (now anticipated) and can be built into policy design. A policy with the ability to adapt to unanticipated conditions can be crafted to:

- accommodate unforeseen issues and changes in context for which the policy was not originally designed, but in ways that support the policy's goals;
- recognize emerging issues that will need to be addressed and
- trigger further analysis and deliberation necessary to make policy adjustments to address emerging issues, maintain performance or terminate the policy if it is no longer relevant.

Based on our review of academic and professional insights for working effectively in complex adaptive systems, on our research of specific policies exhibiting adaptive and maladaptive features, and on interviews with persons impacted by policy, we observe that the capacity of a policy to adapt to anticipated and unanticipated conditions can be facilitated using the following seven tools:

1. *Integrated and forward-looking analysis*—By identifying key factors that affect policy performance and identifying scenarios for how these factors might evolve in the future, policies can be made robust to a range of anticipated conditions, and indicators developed to help trigger important policy adjustments when needed.
2. *Multi-stakeholder deliberation*—A collective and collaborative public effort to examine an issue from different points of view prior to taking a decision, deliberative processes strengthen policy design by building recognition of common values, shared commitment and emerging issues, and by providing a comprehensive understanding of causal relationships.
3. *Automatic policy adjustment*—Some of the inherent variability in socio-economic and ecological conditions can be anticipated, and monitoring of key indicators can help trigger important policy adjustments to keep the policy functioning well.
4. *Enabling self-organization and social networking*—Ensuring that policies do not undermine existing social capital; creating forums that enable social networking; facilitating the sharing of good practices and removing barriers to self-organization—all strengthen the ability of stakeholders to respond to unanticipated events in a variety of innovative ways.

5. **Decentralization of decision-making**—Decentralizing the authority and responsibility for decision-making to the lowest effective and accountable unit of governance, whether existing or newly created, can increase the capacity of a policy to perform successfully when confronted with unforeseen events.

6. **Promoting variation**—Given the complexity of most policy settings, implementing a variety of policies to address the same issue increases the likelihood of achieving desired outcomes. Diversity of responses also forms a common risk-management approach, facilitating the ability to perform efficiently in the face of unanticipated conditions.

7. **Formal policy review and continuous learning**—Regular review, even when the policy is performing well, and the use of well-designed pilots throughout the life of the policy to test assumptions related to performance, can help address emerging issues and trigger important policy adjustments.

The seven tools are presented in Figure 2.2. Most policy design processes begin in a similar manner—by defining the policy, including understanding the issue, setting the policy goal(s), identifying performance indicators and targets and developing policy options. The foundation for the capacity of a policy to adapt to anticipated conditions is formulated in this policy set-up stage. A necessary prerequisite for adaptive policy-making includes identifying the key factors that affect policy performance, articulating scenarios for how the key factors might evolve in the future and testing policy performance under the scenarios (Chapter 3 on integrated and forward-looking analysis). Analytically, policy-makers can gain perspective by studying the past (that is, respecting history), looking forward (that is, scenario outlooks) and understanding the various dimensions of sustainable development (that is, environmental, social and economic). These analytical perspectives are most accurate when a deliberative process is employed with a range of stakeholders and experts (Chapter 4 on multi-stakeholder deliberation), which has the added purpose of building trust, consensus and identity among stakeholders and policy-makers.

It is in the policy design and implementation phase where a policy is made adaptive to anticipated and unanticipated conditions (Figure 2.2). In building a policy's capacity to perform under a range of anticipated conditions, a policy can be designed to perform two functions. First, it is sometimes possible to select policy instruments or to include certain features in a policy instrument that enable it to perform well under a range of anticipated conditions, even worst case, with little or no adjustment. For example, incorporating wind

Figure 2.2   A Framework for Adaptive Policies and Roadmap to this Guidebook

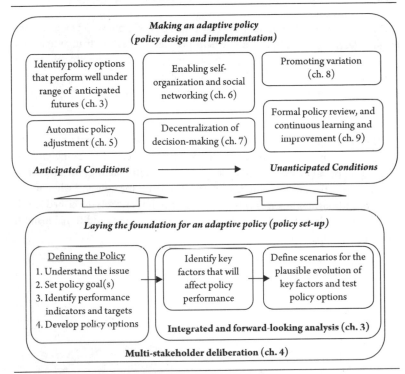

and other renewable energy sources into a hydro-electric power grid reduces the risk associated with extreme drought. Second, a policy can incorporate automatic mechanisms that trigger important pre-defined policy adjustments at the appropriate time, or that trigger further analysis to define the necessary policy adjustment (Chapter 5 on automatic policy adjustment).

For building the capacity of a policy to perform in the face of unanticipated circumstances, we have observed the following as among the most frequently cited leverage points for interacting with complex adaptive systems and were readily detected in our policy research: enabling self-organization and social networking (Chapter 6), decentralizing decision-making to the lowest and most effective jurisdictional level (Chapter 7) and promoting variation in policy responses (Chapter 8). The process of multi-stakeholder deliberation (Chapter 4) is also important as it generates the social and political conditions needed for responding to unanticipated conditions. The linkages among these three mechanisms are many. For example, self-organization and social networking can foster variation in responses, as can decentralization of decision-making.

Last, but certainly not least, formal processes of policy review and continuous learning and improvement help policies to deal with unanticipated issues. This involves time- and stakeholder-triggered reviews for detecting emerging issues and for developing and making timely policy adjustments (Chapter 9). Formal policy review also provides the space in which to pilot test policy instruments and learn lessons with regard to intended outcomes and efficient implementation.

The chapters that follow elaborate on the framework presented earlier by explaining each of the seven tools that we have observed to be helpful for making adaptive policies. Each of Chapters 3 through 9 defines the respective tool, provides the rationale for its use, gives guidance for how and when to use the tool and clarifies linkages with other adaptive policy tools described in this book. We conclude the book with a chapter that provides additional insights for implementing adaptive policies.

3 Integrated and Forward-looking Analysis

Darren Swanson and Sanjay Tomar

What is integrated and forward-looking analysis?
By identifying key factors that affect policy performance and identifying scenarios for how these factors
might evolve in the future, policies can be made robust
to a range of anticipated conditions, and indicators
can be developed to help trigger important policy
adjustments when needed.

WHY IS INTEGRATED AND FORWARD-LOOKING ANALYSIS IMPORTANT FOR CREATING ADAPTIVE POLICIES?

To illustrate the importance of integrated and forward-looking analysis, consider a long-standing, regulated tariff for transporting grain from the Canadian
Prairies to ports for export. The regulated tariff was known as the Crow Rate
and was implemented by the Canadian government from 1897 through 1995.
It initially supported railway expansion in western Canada at the turn of the
19th century.

A largely unanticipated outcome of the Crow Rate's persistence well into
the 20th century was serious under-investment in grain handling and rail
transportation infrastructure—shortcomings brought into stark view when
major grain sales to Russia and China in the 1960s almost caused the system
to collapse. The near-failure of the grain transportation system catalyzed
a flurry of public commissions and inquiries during the period 1960–82 to
investigate and reform the system. The failure to consider the effects of rising
inflation on the performance of the fixed Crow Rate would prove to be one of
the main culprits.

Public pressure eventually catalyzed a complete overhaul of the policy in the form of the Western Grain Transportation Act (WGTA).[1] Following several decades of deterioration in the grain transport system, the lesson with regard to the importance of identifying key policy parameters and how they might evolve in the future had been learned (Swanson and Venema, 2006). The rate would no longer be fixed, calculated with few inputs. The new WGTA policy would consider a range of input parameters in the determination of the freight rate. For example, grain volume forecasts would be provided by the Grain Transportation Agency and the estimated costs to the railways for moving grain would be calculated by the National Transportation Agency (Producer Payment Panel, 1994). This information allowed for the policy to be made more robust to anticipated future conditions. For example, the freight rate would now: include the railways' cost of moving grain and intended to cover variable costs plus 20 per cent towards constant costs (five to six times former levels); and be distance based, designed to allow equal rates for equal distances (ibid.). Additionally, rates would be adjusted each year based on changes to the railways' costs resulting from inflation and grain volume.

Examples of unsuccessful policy interventions such as the story described in the foregoing are common in every country. It is not surprising then to know that there has emerged a great deal of policy literature calling for a more comprehensive, integrated and forward-looking analysis of key factors and drivers that affect policy performance. For example, in creating a toolbox for improving health in cities, Glouberman et al. (2003) paid close attention to integrated assessment. These researchers were armed with the understanding that 'complex adaptive systems are shaped by their past and knowledge of this history may suggest constraints on and opportunities on what can be done in the future'. While this principle of *respecting history* is certainly a glimpse into the obvious, respecting history is perhaps the least respected principle in today's policy-making process. This involves more than simply conducting a trend analysis of existing data that looks back several years. But rather it is about understanding the context and drivers for the issue of concern, and this may require going back not just several years, but several decades, and even several centuries, to understand how society adapted to its present surroundings and its interaction with neighbours.

In his seminal research on adaptive assessment and management for natural resources, Holling (1978) stresses the critical importance of adaptive

---

[1] The Western Grain Transportation Act was terminated in 2001 amidst high grain prices and a declining tolerance for an administered rate in a free-market system.

management and policy design 'which integrates environmental with economic and social understanding at the very beginning of the design process, in a sequence of steps during the design phase and after implementation'. This need to consider the multitude of interactions as a precursor to policy intervention has also been acknowledged in the healthcare sector. Glouberman et al. (2003) note that clearly 'health is not just a function of the individual's biological characteristics, but is profoundly affected by interactions with the natural, built and social environments'.

System properties such as the organized connection between parts, spatial heterogeneity, resilience and dynamic variability, provide the rationale for the recommendations of Holling (1978) to determine significant connections rather than measure everything. With similar rationale, Ruitenbeek and Cartier (2001) in studying processes for adaptive co-management in the forestry sector tell us that policy intervention in complex adaptive systems demands that we *look for linkages in unusual places.*

WHAT IS INTEGRATED AND FORWARD-LOOKING ANALYSIS?

Integrated and forward-looking analysis offers policy-makers a way to view policy design retrospectively, prospectively and comprehensively. These types of analyses are embodied in an approach referred to as scenario planning. A scenario planning approach requires a policy-maker to understand the array of factors that are important to policy performance and which of these factors are most uncertain. It is an effective means for a policy-maker to craft a policy that is robust in a range of plausible future conditions.

Popularized by Royal Dutch Shell in the 1970s, scenarios are 'frameworks for structuring executive's perceptions about alternative future environments in which their decisions might play out' (Ralston and Wilson, 2006). The benefits of scenario analysis and planning in the public policy setting are many. For example, they can provide a decision-maker with:

- an integrated approach to thinking about our environment—a practical means for linking comprehensive, contradictory and incomplete information;
- a better understanding of the dynamics of change that we must address;
- clues as to the timing and nature of key moments of change, where one scenario becomes more likely than another to emerge;

- a fuller range of opportunities and threats, and variety of possible futures to think through their implications;
- an understanding of the formative forces of the future to increase our ability to perceive a wider range of strategic opportunities that might emerge;
- transparency of decision-making—given that the rationale underlying scenarios are readily available to managers who wish to use them;
- a thorough assessment of risks;
- a sound basis for continuous monitoring of the environment (broadly speaking) and strategy adjustment and
- strategies that exhibit a greater degree of resilience and flexibility (Ralston and Wilson, 2006).

The latter two points are particularly noteworthy for adaptive policy-making. Strategies and policies which emerge from scenario planning will have been *tested against a set of scenarios* and *contingency plans* developed along with *triggers* to set contingency plans in motion at the necessary point in time.

Royal Dutch Shell's use of scenarios spawned a range of applications in business, global governance and policy-making. In the corporate sector, Royal Dutch Shell continues to use scenario analysis for strategic management, as do other corporations such as Nokia, and guidance on how to use scenarios in such settings have been developed (for example, Ralston and Wilson, 2006; Schwartz, 1991). Scenarios have also been used extensively in studying global environmental issues. Examples include the United Nations Environment Programme's (UNEP) Global Environment Outlook reports (GEO, 1997, 1999, 2002, 2008) and the Millennium Ecosystem Assessment (MA, 2005). Guidance for the development and analysis of scenarios for such environmental and sustainable development applications has been developed as part of the UNEP Global Environment Outlook process (Jäger et al., 2008).

But the application that we are most interested in for this chapter is policy-making. The scenario planning approach for policy-making follows a similar methodology to scenario planning for corporate strategic management. Examples of scenario analysis in policy-making are not near as prevalent as they are for corporate planning. One example that we learned of during our research was the Ontario Ministry of Education in Canada in their *Schooling for Tomorrow Project* (Glouberman, 2007). As part of one set of experiments with the approach, a series of two workshops were convened which considered a specific policy design case study, raising the mandatory school leaving age from 16 years of age to 18. A diverse study advisory group was assembled to test the approaches and included educators, bureaucrats, administrators, academics, lawyers, political advisors and union leaders from across Canada. For the workshops, individuals from a broad range of positions and constituencies, such as education, labour, health and communications, contributed from across North America.

The day-long policy workshops used scenarios originally developed by the Organisation for Economic Co-operation and Development (OECD) for education and asked participants to examine this policy in the context of each of the five future scenarios using the following questions: 'Would this policy make sense in this scenario?' 'How would you change it?' 'How would the policy affect teachers and teaching in this scenario?' and 'What other policies would you consider or introduce in this scenario?' Feedback from the workshops demonstrated that examining a policy design question using future scenarios was 'extremely useful and stimulating in terms of generating discussion and adding rigour to examining the robustness of policy ideas' (Glouberman, 2007). The advisory group observed that the approach gave workshop participants 'a sense of the complex, imperfect and sometimes disordered political and socio-economic context in which actual policy development emerges'. Glouberman (2007) notes that the scenario analysis approach added a 'fresh dimension to the discussion by recognizing the multiple perspectives that contribute to policy decisions'.

We advocate that scenario analysis and planning for adaptive policy-making can be undertaken based on guidance developed for corporate scenario planning exercises. The basic steps of a scenario planning methodology as outlined by Ralston and Wilson (2006) are outlined in Table 3.1. In the next section we draw on some of these steps to provide guidance for how to use scenario planning in adaptive policy-making (as summarized in Table 3.2).

HOW TO USE INTEGRATED AND FORWARD-LOOKING ANALYSIS IN ADAPTIVE POLICY-MAKING

The scenario planning process fits nicely with the policy design process because the critically important first step in both is clarification. For example, policy set-up typically involves setting policy goal(s), identifying performance indicators and targets, and selecting policy options to consider (Figure 3.1). Advancing more formally into the scenario planning process, the next step is typically to identify the key factors and higher level drivers that affect policy performance. These key factors are then assessed in terms of their relative

Table 3.1   Guidance for Developing and Using Scenarios

Getting Started

Step 1:   Developing the case for scenarios
Step 2:   Gaining executive understanding, support and participation
Step 3:   Defining the 'decision focus'
Step 4:   Designing the process
Step 5:   Selecting the facilitator
Step 6:   Forming the scenario team

Laying the Environmental-Analysis Foundation

Step 7:   Gathering available data, views and projections
Step 8:   Identifying and assessing the key decision factors
Step 9:   Identifying the critical forces and drivers (the dynamics of 'the way the world might work')
Step 10: Conducting focused research on key issues, forces and drivers

Creating the Scenarios

Step 11: Assessing the importance and predictability or uncertainty of forces and drivers
Step 12: Identifying key 'axes of uncertainty' (forces and drivers with high importance and high uncertainty) to serve as logic and structure of the scenarios
Step 13: Selecting scenario logics to cover the 'envelope of uncertainty'
Step 14: Writing the story lines of the scenarios

Moving from Scenarios to a Decision

Step 15: Rehearsing the future with scenarios
Step 16: Getting to the decision recommendations
Step 17: Identifying the signposts to monitor
Step 18: Communicating the results to the organization

Source: Ralston and Wilson, 2006.

Figure 3.1   Adaptive Policy-making for Anticipated Conditions and the Role of Integrated and Forward-looking Analysis

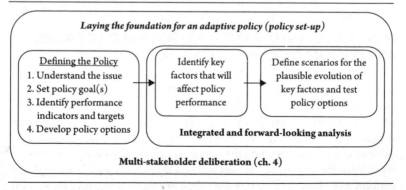

importance to policy performance and also their relative uncertainty in terms of how they might evolve in the future. Factors that are most important and most *certain* become a focus for risk analysis. Factors that are most important and most *uncertain* become the focus for scenario analysis. This latter step is the primary linkage and entry point to adaptive policy-making. It is important to note here that these activities produce the best results when they are done using a deliberative process with multiple stakeholders (the focus of Chapter 4).

The most important and uncertain key factors are then analyzed further to understand the higher-level drivers that could result in changes over time in these factors. It is through this understanding of drivers and their relation to each of the key factors that a set of coherent narratives of plausible futures for the key factors begins to surface. These coherent narratives consist of packets of key factors that all evolve in concert with the drivers. In essence what is created is a set of *policy wind tunnels* in which the performance of a policy can be assessed through qualitative and quantitative analysis. If the policy outcomes under a particular scenario (that is, policy wind tunnel) do not perform in relation to established targets for success, then a series of policy design questions are addressed in order to formulate an adaptive policy (described later in this chapter).

The main steps in the scenario process outlined earlier are discussed in more detail in the paragraphs that follow.

Identifying Key Factors that Affect Policy Performance

Identifying the key factors that affect policy performance is best accomplished in a deliberative process with multiple stakeholders and experts who are involved in implementation of the policy and who are impacted (positively or negatively) by the policy.

An example of the results of such an analysis of key factors is the minimum support price instrument for Agriculture Price Policy (APP) in Punjab, India. The APP was initiated by the government to provide protection to agricultural producers against any sharp drop in farm prices (Mitra and Sareen, 2006). If there is a good harvest and market prices tend to dip, the government guarantees a minimum support price (MSP) or floor price to farmers, which covers not only the cost of production, but also ensures a reasonable profit margin for the producers.

The minimum support prices for major agricultural products are announced each year after taking into account the recommendations of the Commission for Agricultural Costs and Prices (CACP). The CACP takes into account all important factors including cost of production, changes in input prices, input/output price parity, trends in market prices, inter-crop price parity, demand and supply situation, parity between prices paid and prices received by farmers.

- *Cost of production*—It is the most tangible factor and takes into account all operational and fixed demands.
- *Changes in input prices*—It has the ability to address an anticipated change in input price.
- *Input/output price parity*—It considers some anticipated uncertainties in the prices and thus facilitates adjustment.
- *Trends in market prices, international market price situation, inter-crop price parity, effect on general price level*—It keeps track of changes in the market and influences the delivery of the policy.
- *Parity between prices paid and prices received by farmers (terms of trade)*— This anticipates a potential disparity and organizes this mechanism to address that.

Among these factors, the cost of production is the most significant one. A meaningful support price policy should have minimum guaranteed prices, which would cover at least the reasonable cost of production in a normal agricultural season obtained from efficient farming. The CACP carries out state-specific analyses for the cost of production in respect of various commodities. This is done through consultations with the state governments. After a meeting of the state chief ministers, the MSP/procurement prices are declared. Cost of production for the same crops varies between regions, across farms within the same region and for different producers. This makes it difficult to have a norm for the level of costs. In fixing the support prices, CACP relies on the cost concept, which covers all items of expenses of cultivation including the imputed value of input owned by farmers such as rental value of owned land and interest on fixed capital.

Scenario analysis and planning goes far beyond just identifying key factors. The next step in the approach takes these key factors further and assesses which are most important and also most uncertain (Jäger et al., 2008; Ralston and Wilson, 2006). A technique used to facilitate this ranking is to ask stakeholders and experts (through consensus) to place each factor on a diagram representing importance versus uncertainty, as illustrated in Figure 3.2. Jäger et al. (2008) describe those factors in the upper right (the most important and uncertain) as the 'critical uncertainties'. These factors form the basis for defining plausible future scenarios. Those factors in the upper left part of the

Figure 3.2   Ranking Key Factors with Respect to Importance and Uncertainty

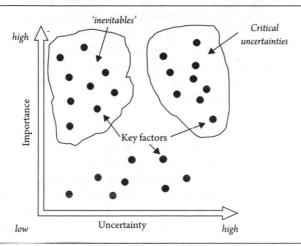

Source: Adapted from Jäger et al. (2008).

diagram are still important, but their future evolution is quite certain. Jäger et al. (2008) refer to these as the '*inevitables*' and these provide context for the scenarios.

Policy Wind Tunnel: Developing Plausible Scenarios for the Evolution of Key Factors

Once the key factors affecting policy performance and critical uncertainties have been identified, the potential future evolution of these key factors can be projected using a combination of qualitative and quantitative methods.

We observed an example of projecting the evolution of an individual key factor in our policy research of the Irrigation District (ID) programme of the Government of Alberta, Canada (Swanson et al., 2008). The St. Mary River Irrigation District (SMRID) in southern Alberta played a leading role in establishing a water sharing agreement between Irrigation Districts, municipalities and industrial water users during the drought year of 2001. Representatives from Alberta Environment and Alberta Agriculture Food and Rural Development (AAFRD) formed a technical advisory committee to the Irrigation Districts and other groups negotiating the sharing agreement. Though not voting members, they attended all meetings to provide information about how priorities might be implemented under a variety of water supply scenarios and about laws and policies (Rush et al., 2004). Through monthly planning sessions, water supply forecasts and water rationing strategies for irrigation and non-irrigation users were formulated. The Irrigation Branch of AAFRD then worked with the IDs and Alberta Environment to calculate estimates of the volume of water that would be available, and were also able to calculate values for each farmer using individual on-farm irrigation system data.

Scenarios, however, are more than just projections of individual key factors. They represent a coherent package of key factors. The coherence is achieved by understanding the higher-level drivers for these key factors and how these drivers influence the various key factors. For example, water availability might be a key factor affecting irrigation potential, and among the drivers of change in this key factor could be global climate change and the demand for food. A coherent scenario of how a range of key factors might evolve in the future is much like a wind tunnel used to test the performance of airplanes and automobiles (Rothman, 2007). This *policy wind tunnel* constructed as a scenario can be used to test the performance of policy with respect to its ability to achieve intended goal(s). Methods are available to help ensure consistency and coherence among key factors within a scenario. Among these are principal components analysis and morphological analysis. These nuanced methods are beyond the scope of this guidebook. Interested readers are referred to Ritchey (2005) for guidance on using morphological analysis in futures studies.

Key Adaptive Policy Design Questions

If the policy outcomes assessed under a particular scenario (that is, in the policy wind tunnel) do not perform well in relation to established targets for success, then the first of three policy design questions should be addressed in order to formulate an adaptive policy.

1. Can a policy option be developed to perform in a range of anticipated future conditions?

This question deals with no-regrets type policy options. These are policies that are likely to work well no matter what anticipated conditions might prevail. Bankes (2002) makes a practical and direct linkage between scenario analysis and adaptive policies. He suggested that 'adaptive policies need to be evaluated on their *robustness properties*, not on their performance on any single case'. He advocates that scenario analysis can be used to find cases that break a proposed policy, and that such worst cases can stimulate policy-makers to modify the range of possible policies to allow for combinations that hedge against these worst cases (ibid.).

Consider an example of hydropower development in the face of increasing drought potential caused by climate change. A risk management strategy in such a case might be to diversify the power supply by developing a source that is uncorrelated to the drought risk. Development of wind power could be a robust policy under such anticipated future conditions. It is an example of something that can be done now that would help the power supply system perform successfully in a range of anticipated future climatic conditions. If costs are similar to hydropower, and the socio-economic and environmental impacts are less than or similar to the existing sources, then this can be considered a no-regrets or robust type of policy for the future.

We observed from our policy research some examples of no-regrets types of policy design in the Canadian province of Manitoba's Crop Insurance Program (Swanson and Venema, 2007). The federal-provincial cost sharing formulas for insurance costs in the Federal Crop Insurance Act includes a feature that allows it to be robust to a range of anticipated future conditions. Two cost sharing formulas were included in the act:

- fifty per cent of a province's incurred administration costs and a maximum of 25 per cent of the total premium costs or
- fifty per cent of the total premium costs if the provincial government pays for all the administration costs.

While most provinces have opted for the second formula, the availability of options reflects a respect for the diversity of circumstances that exist among the provinces implementing crop insurance programmes.

We observed another example of robust policy design in the calculation of average yield for determining indemnities in the Manitoba Crop Insurance Program. The Federal-Provincial Crop Insurance Review Committee describes that the average yield is determined for different geographic areas having common soil, climate, production and risk characteristics. Within each risk area in the province, 'base premium rates and yields are adjusted according to soil productivity levels' (FPCIR, 1989: 25). The soils are actually grouped into anywhere from 6–15 soil productivity classes and a simple multiplicative indices or comparative rating system is applied to each class to end up with productivity ratings.

The review committee goes on to note that risk is related to yield variability, and as such, emphasis should be placed on variability and probability, rather than mean. They state: 'the suitability of the simple average yield to fully represent probable crop yield is being questioned, particularly due to the rapidly increasing yield potential being made possible for some crops by emerging technology' (ibid.). Related to the yield estimation is the flexibility to account for experience in crop insurance payouts gained in certain regions. Where experience is available, average yields are based on the productive capability of the individuals (FPCIR, 1989: 15).

The second policy design question relates to assessing vulnerability in relation to unintended outcomes.

2. What are the potential adverse and unintended impacts of the policy and what actions can be taken now to mitigate or hedge against the consequences?

Walker et al. (2001), in the context of transportation policy issues, point out that adverse consequences 'can reduce acceptance of the policy to the point where success is jeopardized'. They cite some vulnerabilities related to expansion plans for Schiphol International Airport in the Netherlands. For example, noise can be a significant adverse consequence of an increase in capacity. They describe *mitigating actions* as possibly including buying out homes in the noise zone, subsidizing sound insulation, subsidizing real estate markets and paying out compensation. Airline accidents are another potential adverse consequence. *Hedging actions* for this vulnerability, they note, could include subsidizing business or residential insurance in the area.

The concept of sustainable development provides a useful framework for helping to ensure that an assessment of the potential adverse consequences of a policy is as comprehensive as possible. In its most basic form, the sustainable development concept asks that an issue be studied from environmental, economic and social perspectives, and that the impact on future generations must also be given full consideration. Sets of questions have been developed to assist policy-makers with analysis of potential impacts from multiple perspectives, including sector-specific applications such as the Criteria for Great Plains Sustainability (IISD, 1993) and the Seven Questions to Sustainability for the mining sector (IISD, 2002).

The third adaptive policy design question relates to future policy adjustments.

3. How might the policy need to be adjusted in the future in order to continue to perform successfully and how will the adjustment be triggered?

Tools for answering this question are discussed in detail in Chapter 5 on automatic adjustment. It is certainly not always the case that a policy option can be devised with little or no modification to perform successfully in a range of anticipated future conditions—the focus of question 1. In such instances, adaptive policy-making requires that critically important modifications to the policy be triggered and implemented at the appropriate point in time. This requires monitoring changes in three types of indicators: (1) the key factors affecting policy performance, such as the rate of inflation in the case of Canada's former Crow Rate for grain transportation; (2) system performance indicators that inform if the policy is achieving its intended goal(s) and (3) indicators that monitor for potential unintended impacts.

Walker et al. (2001), and Walker and Marchau (2003) refer to such indicators as signposts. When a key factor affecting policy performance moves outside the range considered in the design of the policy, a policy adjustment or reassessment is triggered. Chapter 5 will discuss the notion of policy adjustment in terms of *fully-automatic* if the precise policy adjustment can be pre-defined, or *semi-automatic* if further analysis is necessary to determine the precise policy adjustment.

WHEN TO USE SCENARIO ANALYSIS FOR ADAPTIVE POLICY-MAKING

Our discussion of scenario analysis in this chapter focuses primarily on its application as a tool to aid in the design of specific policies once the policy goals have been clarified and successful performance defined. Application of scenarios under such conditions is commonly referred to as scenario planning. It should be noted, however, that scenario analysis can also be used at a much higher level for helping to identify policy goals that can lead to favourable futures. The latter is an application of scenario analysis that would precede the first box in the framework illustrated in Figure 3.1 (for example., before setting specific policy goals). For guidance on this type of scenario analysis we refer you to the scenario analysis module in the Global Environment Outlook Resource Book on Integrated Environmental Assessment and Reporting (Jäger et al., 2008).

The point in the policy cycle regarding the application of the type of scenario analysis discussed in this chapter is during policy design—just after the policy has been identified and its goal specified. In this context, scenario analysis is about creating *policy wind tunnels*, to test policy performance under a range of anticipated conditions. For example, in a pseudo scenario analysis we saw in the example of the SMRID in Alberta, Canada that water supply forecasts were developed early on in design of the water sharing agreement before the government estimated water use values for each farmer. For the minimum support price example in India, an integrated assessment of key policy parameters informed the array of parameters necessary to determine an effective price.

In the case where either *fully* or *semi-automatic* policy adjustments are prescribed (see Chapter 5), scenario analysis is an ongoing process of monitoring and policy adaptation. What we advocate in this chapter is a shorter and more focused application of an often longer and more involved scenario analysis process used to help set priorities for action within a much broader government mandate.

The scenario analysis process is subject to several constraints such as the time and capacity available for policy-makers to undertake it. The availability of data can also be a constraint on the utility of scenarios in helping to craft adaptive policies. The inherent constraint with scenario analysis in relation to adaptive policy-making is that it is limited by what we can anticipate. Even if we do the most comprehensive scenario analysis that money can buy, the unknown unknowns still exist. Axelrod and Cohen (2000) note that the scenario analysis process is 'hobbled' if we cannot address the key questions related to uncertainty. So this approach should be combined with mechanisms for dealing with unanticipated issues (see Chapters 6 through 9).

LINKS TO OTHER ADAPTIVE POLICY TOOLS

The most obvious linkage with the other adaptive policy tools listed in this guidebook is the one with automatic policy adjustment (Chapter 5). The key factors which are identified through scenario analysis, along with the process of articulating plausible evolutions of the factors, makes it possible to craft automatic adjustment mechanisms.

Rotmans (1998) notes that there is a general understanding in the professional integrated assessment community that, while participation of stakeholders is not a prerequisite for conducting an integrated assessment, it 'significantly improves the quality of the assessment by giving access to practical knowledge and experience and to a wider range of perspectives and options'. It is a general consensus among practitioners that the results of a scenario analysis are highly dependent on the range of perspectives that are drawn on during the process. Therefore, multi-stakeholder deliberation (Chapter 4) is an important element of any scenario analysis and planning process. In addition to providing the necessary intellectual input, the deliberative process in scenario analysis serves to build awareness among stakeholders of plausible future conditions, and builds trust among the participants that policy decisions are being made in a thoughtful manner.

Table 3.2 Overview of Integrated and Forward-looking Analysis for Adaptive Policy-making

Integrated and forward-looking analysis: By identifying key factors that affect policy performance and identifying scenarios for how these factors might evolve in the future, policies can be made robust to a range of anticipated conditions, and indicators developed to help trigger important policy adjustments when needed.

Why?	What is it?	How to apply it?	When to use it?
• To respect history (Glouberman et al, 2003). • To understand interactions with the natural, built and social environment (ibid.). • To look for linkages in unusual places (Ruitenbeek and Cartier, 2001). • To place efforts in determining significant connections rather than measuring everything (Holling, 1978). • To understand local conditions and strengths and assets (Glouberman et al, 2003).	Scenarios are 'frameworks for structuring executive's perceptions about alternative future environments in which their decisions might play out' (Ralston and Wilson, 2006). Scenario planning is a deliberative and iterative process that: identifies key factors affecting performance; articulates coherent scenarios for how key factors might evolve in the future; tests plans/policies for how they might perform under different scenarios; identifies actions to improve performance, and monitors progress.	**Identifying key factors that affect policy performance** Best accomplished in a deliberative process with multiple stakeholders, experts involved in implementation of the policy, and those who are impacted (positively or negatively) by the policy. **Creating the policy wind tunnel—developing scenarios for the plausible evolution of key factors** Potential future evolution of the key factors can be projected using a combination of qualitative and quantitative methods. Scenarios are a coherent package of key factors. Coherence is achieved by understanding the higher-level drivers for these key factors and how these drivers influence the various key factors. **Addressing key adaptive policy design questions** 1. Can a policy option be developed to perform in a range of anticipated future conditions? 2. What are the potential adverse and unintended impacts of the policy and what actions can be taken now to mitigate and hedge against the consequences? 3. How might the policy need to be adjusted in the future in order to continue to perform successfully and how will the adjustment be triggered?	Scenario planning for adaptive policy-making is applied in the policy design phase after a policy has been identified and the goal(s) set.

The adaptive policy mechanism of formal policy review and continuous learning (Chapter 9) for addressing unanticipated conditions is also closely linked with scenario analysis and planning. The formal review process can revisit the scenarios that were developed to help detect emerging issues. This is made possible because effort is expended while defining scenarios to understand the potential causal linkages among key factors and among their higher-level drivers.

4 Multi-stakeholder Deliberation

Stephen Tyler

What is multi-stakeholder deliberation? Multi-stakeholder deliberation is a collective and collaborative public effort to examine an issue from different points of view prior to taking a decision. Deliberative processes strengthen policy design by building recognition of common values, shared commitment and emerging issues, and by providing a comprehensive understanding of causal relationships.

WHY IS DELIBERATION IMPORTANT FOR ADAPTIVE POLICY?

Adaptive natural resource policies need to accommodate the diversity and dynamics of local biophysical conditions, as well as the unexpected trajectories of preference and social response to change. This means that decision-makers should recognize the dimensions of diverse experience, knowledge and user needs. In a complex and rapidly evolving world, public deliberation provides access to diverse and innovative perspectives and helps ensure adaptive responses (Roberts, 2004).

The conventional approach to natural resource management policy has been to control certain factors so as to optimize the performance of the resource system. For example, we may want to optimize the production of timber and fibre from forests, or we may want to optimize the yield of grain from agriculture, or minimize flooding. Policies and interventions are designed sectorally. Interventions such as engineering infrastructure, fertilizers and other inputs, or land management practices are adjusted with this limited range of optimization targets in mind. However, our ability to predict the evolution of complex social-ecological systems is not very good. The boundaries and performance of ecosystems do not conform to those of single sectors or jurisdictions. Social priorities also shift with time, although fundamental values and interests tend to be more persistent (Walker and Salt, 2006).

For all these reasons, adaptive natural resource policies should be built on more than just careful data collection, scientific and technical analysis, and predictive modelling of key parameters—approaches that were discussed in Chapter 3. *Multi-stakeholder deliberation* provides a tool for engaging not only the opinions and values of different interests, but also different kinds of knowledge and different ways of knowing (Haas, 1992). The benefits of this approach are not purely instrumental: that is, this is not just about getting the policy 'right' or ensuring legitimacy. The outcome of deliberation is not abstract generalization, or discrete policy decisions, but meanings shared by the participants and narratives that engage their own accounts of success or failure (Forester, 1999). Participatory processes are not merely about being heard or about negotiation or about sharing evidence and building consensus on facts (although all these are important) but crucially about political identity, about values, about building social cohesion and competence, mutual respect, hope and capacity to act collectively. Such processes, though time consuming, have crucial transformative potential in creating new, shared vision that can motivate learning and policy adaptation. Building a sense of shared values and interests through public deliberation, particularly in a context of potential or real social conflict, is also helpful to prepare for the *effective implementation* of adaptive policies. Political theorists argue that the process of deliberation builds civic confidence, participation and trust in democratic governance, in addition to informing policy design (Delli Carpini et al., 2004).

Public deliberation is thus important for adaptive policies in two ways. First, it provides access to different perspectives, different sources of knowledge and different ways of knowing in order to consider new information and new views of the problem. In this way, it expands the ability of policy design to incorporate a range of anticipated conditions. Second, but equally important, it builds the social cohesion, shared vision and capacity for collective action that are essential to enable rapid adjustment and response to unanticipated conditions.

The importance of deliberative processes at the local decision-making level can be seen in the experience of Hiwre Bazaar village in Maharashtra state in India. In a case study of community adaptation, the capacity of this village to adapt to climatic variability was illustrated to be demonstrably greater than other rainfed villages. Residents required less recourse to debt, and were able to maintain food stocks and production even in drought conditions, despite having only limited access to irrigation. The main differentiating factors were the village's strong leadership and deliberative processes for investment in water harvesting, irrigation management, introducing new cropping systems (even when these were not popular) and sharing lessons to spread innovations. The engagement of multiple perspectives at the village level, and the deliberation of evidence and experience in making choices, provided opportunities for social learning essential to strengthening resilience and adaptation (Bhadwal, 2008).

This chapter discusses what we mean by multi-stakeholder deliberation, its strengths and limitations, so as to provide some guidelines about how it can best be used to make public policy more adaptive, and then shares some examples of good practice in relation to natural resources management. An overview of multi-stakeholder deliberation as an adaptive policy tool is provided in Table 4.1.

WHAT IS MULTI-STAKEHOLDER DELIBERATION?

Public deliberation of policy decisions is an ancient practice, famously formalized in the *agora* of Athens. It is still in common use, but in today's world of huge bureaucracies, technologically complex choices, professional lobbyists and highly trained public administrators, proponents of an administrative model of the modern state argue that professional administrators are better placed to make decisions and more accountable to elected representatives. The public is commonly depicted as misinformed, apathetic, unskilled in communicating or learning about policy decisions, and often outright intolerant and anti-democratic. This perspective leaves ordinary citizens a very limited legitimate role in public decision-making. On the other hand, a pluralist model of the state suggests that citizens have as much right to advocate for their interests as do large corporations and interest groups, and direct-democracy theorists would argue that in certain conditions citizens ought to take responsibility themselves for policy decision-making (Roberts, 2004).

Deliberation is commonly defined as 'discussion and consideration by a group of persons (as a jury or legislature) of the reasons for and against a measure'.[1] The term implies the reasoned consideration of evidence, careful forethought prior to decisions and looking at different sides of an issue. In the context of public decision-making, the term implies a collective and collaborative effort to examine an issue from different points of view in order to share learning and build consensus prior to taking a decision.

---

[1] http://www.m-w.com/dictionary/deliberation

We have chosen to make explicit the requirement that this process engages in multiple perspectives to highlight the risk of structuring a consultative or deliberative process so as to reduce, rather than enhance, diverse engagement. Deliberative processes are always prone to manipulation because it is easier and quicker to make decisions if the range of input is limited or the legitimacy of alternative views is undermined.

In political theory, public deliberation focuses on the communicative processes that form public opinion and public will, rather than on voting processes by which that will is exercised. Accountability in deliberative democracy means being able to give a satisfactory public account that justifies public policy, rather than necessarily facing a vote. Public deliberation is thus not depicted as an alternative to representative democracy, but as an extension of it (Chambers, 2003, cited in Delli Carpini et al., 2004).

We are not referring here to broad informal policy discourse, or discourse mediated by elites or public media. Rather this is a carefully structured opportunity for groups of people representing different social interests and perspectives to engage in reflection, interaction and learning. This is close to what Daniels and Walker (1996) call 'Collaborative Learning', combining elements of Soft Systems Methodology (using systems principles and learning processes to re-frame complex problems and explore alternative solutions); and Alternative Dispute Resolution (dealing with strategic behaviour and value differences in conflict situations).

Based on the literature reviewing public deliberation practice, its links to political and cognitive theory, and its application to natural resources management, we can describe the following characteristics of an effective multi-stakeholder deliberation process:

- Participation is voluntary (ibid.).
- The effort is structured and led by skilled facilitators. Deliberative processes can exacerbate conflict and public alienation if mishandled (Delli Carpini et al., 2004; Ryfe, 2005).
- The process is guided by explicit rules and procedures (these are discussed in next section).
- All participants have an opportunity to speak, and all should feel that their views have been heard and considered without risk or prejudice. The process is structured to accommodate and respect—even to value—plural perspectives (Roberts, 2004). While deliberative processes are not generally designed to negotiate conflicts, they should be able to handle conflicting views and negotiation of common interests.

- Participants include a broad range of stakeholders directly or indirectly affected by the decision. Social groups who might otherwise be marginalized from decision-making should be explicitly engaged (Arnstein, 1969; Roberts, 2004). Special provisions may be needed for support to ensure such groups can participate in a reasonably egalitarian fashion (depending on the culture and context, there could be need for translation, compensation for lost wages, transportation, childcare, and so on).
- Deliberative proceedings are transparent and accessible. There can be good reasons for keeping some kinds of deliberative discussions private, so as to enable individual participants to adjust their positions on the basis of learning and exchange, without having to posture as representatives of specific public positions. But the information inputs, the procedural guidelines and the results of deliberation should always be public and, in most cases, the entire proceedings are.
- Multi-stakeholder deliberation is a social learning process. Participants engage each other on the basis of communication and open discussion. Arguments are de-personalized, assumptions and evidence are held up for reflection and criticism. Perspectives and positions change with learning (Daniels and Walker, 1996; Ryfe, 2005).
- Deliberation is aimed at an explicit decision context. It is not intended merely to generate opinions. Participants should be confident that their inputs will have a direct bearing on policy decision-making, even if recommendations are not accepted in their entirety (Roberts, 2004).
- Deliberation is most effective when conducted face-to-face. This has clear implications for the size of group that can effectively interact. If the group gets much larger than 20, the effectiveness of the activity breaks down. Large group deliberations require careful organization and subdivision into smaller sub-groups (Delli Carpini et al., 2004; Roberts, 2004).

Deliberation is a process that jars people out of the typical cognitive short-cuts by which they normally frame day-to-day problems. Because of this, it may provoke frustration and anxiety, particularly if the process generates no new 'short-cuts' or simple solutions (Ryfe, 2005). As a result, it is important that participants be motivated. Cognitive and cultural theory suggests that when the decisions are important and the participants have a meaningful stake in the outcome (that is, stakes are high and the stakeholders are at the table), they are likely to be more motivated. In addition, motivation is enhanced by accountability to others, by a sense of threatened interests and by engagement with others who have different perspectives (ibid.). All these factors are socially and culturally constructed, therefore the nature of deliberative processes must match its social and cultural context.

For example, the promotion of zero-tillage practices in the province of Saskatchewan, Canada, was accomplished in part through government research and also through farmer/extension groups. Deliberative discussions enabled farmers to critically examine both scientific and experiential evidence together, and legitimized new techniques more rapidly than classic technical advisory services would have. In this case, the decision focus of the deliberative process was not on a policy decision, but on a business decision: whether farmers should invest in direct-seeding equipment, chemicals and zero-tillage practices. The results of the deliberative process were changed attitudes and behaviours of farmers, leading to more adaptive farming practices. Public deliberation among members of the extension association also led to the adoption of carbon sequestration as an innovative application of the technique, responsive to emerging policy and market opportunities.

One of the premises of multi-stakeholder deliberation in natural resources management is that approaches to complex social and resource management problems are not 'given', but have to be co-learned. In fact, deliberation is not about narrowly responsive problem-solving as much as exploring new approaches, fostering shared learning and building consensus (Roberts, 1997). It is not a process driven by technical experts, although the information provided by science and technical research is often very valuable in deliberative processes, where it can be exposed and examined critically for its implications.

There are many examples of the role of deliberation in fostering collective action for adaptive natural resources management. Often, the engagement of different perspectives can lead to the adoption of completely different objectives for a programme, or to insights that directly inform more adaptive policies. For example, a study of community forestry in the Philippines, when it engaged the community in deliberation of the situation, was completely reorganized in recognition that researchers had mis-diagnosed the problems. The subsequent project used deliberation techniques extensively to transform entrenched conflicts and influence policy change (O'Hara, 2006).

HOW TO USE MULTI-STAKEHOLDER DELIBERATION IN ADAPTIVE POLICY-MAKING

As with many of the tools discussed in this guidebook, multi-stakeholder deliberation can be used in various ways. However, in order to address the challenges outlined earlier, practitioners need to pay attention to procedural details. Key aspects that need to be addressed in implementing deliberative mechanisms include:

Preparation

- Basic procedural issues of sponsorship, facilitation, leadership, decision-making, sequencing, support requirements and follow-up need to be clarified by organizers. The larger the numbers of people involved in the deliberative exercise, and the more complex the decision context, the more attention needs to be paid to these issues (Roberts, 2004).
- Decision rules need to be agreed in advance. Consensus works best if there are strongly shared interests, participants are known to each other and are members of the same community, and a single best solution is logically possible. Voting may be better when underlying interests diverge sharply, or participants do not know each other well and share a community or common commitment. No single best solution will satisfy in any event. Both decision rules need to be used contextually (Delli Carpini et al., 2004).
- Face-to-face deliberation is most effective in changing attitudes or opinions, research suggests. Conversation is a more powerful form of communicating trust and emotion, which are key elements in convincing others and in assessing whether others listen to your inputs. This helps to build legitimacy, which is an important factor to ensure social learning and eventual collaborative follow-up (ibid.).

Participant Selection

- Participant selection should ensure the engagement of marginal groups because of the pervasiveness of power differentials. Voluntary self-selection is important to benefit from the energy of those most engaged, but is insufficient without some mechanism to bring in other voices. A purely random selection process can be very costly and time consuming, so some kind of purposive sampling is normally used.
- Stakeholders who are included in a process from the beginning become more invested in the process and its outcomes than those who are merely asked to select from among a set of options (Forester, 1999).

Deliberation

- The process relies on effective communications, but such skills are not widespread. Therefore, the deliberative process needs to help participants build communication competencies such as skills in listening; non-threatening questioning and clarification; feedback; social cognition and dialogue (Daniels and Walker, 1996).
- Leadership is vital. Participants take cues from leaders who model reflective, respectful and open language, and are demonstrably willing to learn and change their own views.
- Social learning is a fundamental aspect of the approach. Shared and collaborative learning is an *active*, not a passive, process: participants should ideally be engaged in doing, not just listening. They need to draw on their experience and the process should engage different modes of thinking: recall experience/narrative; reflection/observation; conceptualization and experimentation. Strategies for participation should be varied to accommodate different learning styles. Learning benefits from systems thinking and from the generation of novelty rather than simply debate of familiar positions (Senge, 1990).

In the province of Manitoba, Canada, policies behind the development of local conservation districts (CDs) did not bestow significant enforcement powers on local authorities for soil and water conservation. Delivery mechanisms relied on local deliberative strategies for shared learning, partnership-building, planning and priority-setting for natural resources management. These mechanisms have had a positive impact on the adaptability of the underlying policy. Despite challenges in addressing the key issue of surface drainage management, the CDs throughout the province have provided a flexible institutional framework for improving natural resources management along a host of unexpected dimensions, because of their decentralized and deliberative structure.

The Whitemud CD in the southwestern part of the province in particular, has adopted practices that ensure appropriate deliberative decision-making, using many of the principles articulated earlier (for example, field meetings that allow open discussion and personal investigation on matters relating to drain licences). Because the Whitemud CD has boundaries consistent with the watershed and authority for drainage management (uniquely in the province; see Chapter 7 for more details), it is better able to organize effective deliberation on key resource management issues. Participants have high stakes in the outcome of deliberations and recognize that a decision can be taken as a result of their inputs. This helps ensure effective participation.

The Manitoba CD policy was flexible enough to accommodate initiatives that arose from local deliberation and the engagement of multiple stakeholders. The multi-stakeholder deliberation of different local partners ensured that the CD remained relevant to resource management issues locally and provided a foundation for continued effectiveness. As a result of these local deliberations, CD mandates shifted, enabling adaptation to unanticipated conditions and local opportunities. These have included various local priority issues: to cap abandoned water wells and protect groundwater supplies; to establish legal agreements to protect privately-owned upland forest lands; or to initiate trans-boundary watershed consultations or partnerships with First Nations groups.

Multi-stakeholder public deliberation in natural resources management applications is also consistent with principles of adaptive co-management. It is based on stakeholder participation; on shared learning; on new roles for resource users, public officials and researchers; on iterative assessment of values and experience together with new knowledge; and on action learning—testing in practice the innovations developed through collaborative deliberation and shared knowledge (Tyler, 2006).

In India, watershed management groups had an impact in Ahmednagar district in Maharashtra state. Locally organized, they provided opportunities for face-to-face deliberation on decisions around water use and adoption of new cropping patterns. They played a significant role in the switch away from sugarcane, despite profitability, and towards less water-intensive vegetables and millet. In this case, the nature of the decisions resulting from deliberation included production decisions by individual farmers and households, collective decisions on land use, investment in water and soil conservation, and shared practices for water use. The case study also explains how leadership can play a role in enhancing policy objectives, encompassing the views of the communities through a public deliberation process (Bhadwal, 2008).

In Maharashtra, the development of deliberative skills and organization is the responsibility of the Project Implementation Agency (PIA). They undertake Participatory Rural Appraisal (PRA) to provide baseline information for exchange and shared learning, develop local organizations to lead and support the deliberative efforts, and contribute technical expertise, scientific knowledge and funding as appropriate to assist in local planning and decision-making on watershed management. The PIA provides oversight mechanisms for audit and validation to boost trust and legitimacy when there is little familiarity with the process and organization. A capacity-building phase of six to eight months is normally required to develop the deliberative skills and decision-making organizational context in the community. This demonstrates the need for skilled support to deliberative processes, and also illustrates the complementary role of analysis and information gathering.

Participatory approaches are clearly recognized under the National Watershed Development Project for Rainfed Areas (NWDPRA) in India (Tomar and Nair, 2008). The formation of self-help groups and other community organizations provides mechanisms for including marginal social groups in local deliberation, shared learning and decision-making on watershed management. Community groups contribute to watershed improvement projects, building local stakes to reinforce motivation for deliberation and participatory decision-making. Local deliberative processes help to ensure that watershed management investments address local barriers to improved resource management, build effective institutions for problem diagnosis and decision-making, and connect to credit and extension services. These factors are significant in building adaptive capacity, strengthening local learning and providing opportunities for innovation and investment.

Intractable conflicts require special tools and processes. Such situations are high-risk and expectations for outcomes need to be managed accordingly. A basic assumption of deliberative decision-making is that it is possible to identify shared values and new insights that can form the basis for common ground.

In the southern region of the province of Alberta, Canada, Irrigation Districts (IDs) constituted under the auspices of recently updated water legislation play a central role in adapting to changes in water availability (Swanson et al., 2008). There are several ways in which multi-stakeholder deliberation has been used by the St. Mary River Irrigation District (SMRID) to guide difficult water resource management decisions. For example, the South Saskatchewan River Basin water management plan provides the policy framework for IDs in southern Alberta, together with other large water users, guiding their priority-setting and water use practices. This plan was the result of a deliberative process involving provincial government agencies, IDs, municipalities and the general public over a period of several years.

The SMRID has deliberated with stakeholders to develop contingency plans for drought, when water will be re-allocated among users, and for flooding, when vulnerability and emergency responses need to be coordinated among small towns, rural areas and senior levels of government.

The examples presented here mostly demonstrate the application of deliberative processes to local-scale decision-making on natural resources management, but these mechanisms can also be employed at the level of senior government policies. Public deliberation on complex national policy issues is difficult to manage effectively because of the need to limit the number of participants, and by the distance between stakeholders and decision-makers. Therefore, it frequently takes the form of some kind of representative forum such as a specially constituted reference group, citizens' assembly or citizens' jury.[2]

The label 'multi-stakeholder' consultation or deliberation is often used to apply to this kind of more limited interaction, often away from public view, between representatives of stakeholder groups in a situation of policy dispute (for example, 'roundtables' on the economy and environment). The differences between these situations and more open and public engagement are important. While they may be more practical, there are also risks in smaller, less transparent stakeholder discussions: elite capture; marginalization; domination of 'conventional' or convergent thinking or a lack of accountability. They should try, as much as possible, to adhere to the same principles as outlined earlier for broader public deliberation in order to avoid these shortcomings.

WHEN TO USE MULTI-STAKEHOLDER DELIBERATION

In relation to the generalized policy cycle introduced in Chapter 2, deliberative approaches are helpful at several stages. They are particularly useful in understanding and framing issues and in setting objectives (that is, 'front end' of policy cycle) because they provide a way to gather and sift through diverse perspectives on complex issues that are hard to define, in order to help resolve what kinds of actions are feasible and appropriate. This improves adaptability because it recognizes that interests can shift, and a policy that addresses multiple interests is more likely to be robust. It also permits tentative policy objectives to be tested against a range of experience, opinion and public positions to build shared vision and commitment. With commitment to shared vision and objectives, policy implementation can be more easily devolved and adapted by local institutions.

Deliberation during these defining stages of the policy cycle also can provide valuable contributions to effective design of adaptive policy later on. It

---

[2] This approach was developed by the Jefferson Center in the US (http://www.jefferson-center. org/) but has been widely applied in the UK and modified by other European countries (http:// www.communityinvolvement.org.uk/new_page_7.htm and http://www.tekno.dk/subpage.php 3?article=1231&toppic=kategori12&language=uk).

not only improves the understanding of key structural relations relevant to policy design, but also clarifies the criteria and conditions of success, so that analysts and practitioners can more readily develop effective monitoring and evaluation programmes.

Deliberation is also useful in the evaluation, learning and adaptation stages of policy implementation. Deliberative processes are especially valuable in the policy learning stage (see Chapter 5 on automatic policy adjustment and Chapter 9 on formal policy review and continuous learning), for the same reasons as noted earlier: different perspectives and interests, as well as different knowledge and experience, and even different epistemic frameworks, all help to assess what is changing in complex systems, how to interpret and respond to it.

Multi-stakeholder deliberation is often employed in situations where decisions are contentious and stakeholders are vocal or well organized. It is also sometimes used in response to situations where there is dissatisfaction with current decision-making. In both cases, this process should only be used if it can be seen to be equitable, accessible and enabling social learning. If it is manipulative, or purely symbolic, the process is likely to generate even greater resentment and polarization.

Deliberation demands new roles of citizens, administrators and technical experts in dialogue and collaboration. Policy decision-makers and executives serve as the facilitators and stewards of this process, and must try to maintain the public trust. This social learning process, uniquely among the many variants of 'public participation', places citizens in a role equal to that of public administrators, as co-learners and partners in decision-making (Daniels and Walker, 1996; Roberts, 2004).

Nor is this a model for simple problem solving. Deliberation generally addresses difficult trade-offs and seeks innovative approaches and consensus measures. Recognizing that many difficult problems do not have solutions, deliberation strives for recognition of the complexities and for improvement in the current situation (Rittel and Webber, 1973). It encourages systems thinking by extending linkages between different problem elements and different social groups, and welcomes non-linear options. It is communication intensive, rather than analytically intensive, but this does not mean analysis is irrelevant to the shared learning process. A deliberative process recognizes that learning is not only intrinsic, but probably needs to continue after the decision is made (Daniels and Walker, 1996; Lee, 1993; Roberts, 1997).

There are many challenges to multi-stakeholder deliberation. The unequal political power of diverse stakeholders can lead to deeper antagonism and mistrust unless there is strong commitment to 'levelling the playing field' for all participants. Arnstein (1969) suggests that enabling the engagement of poor and marginalized social groups in deliberative decision-making will improve the quality of decisions, build ownership of outcomes and strengthen their legitimacy.

There are also challenges of scale, especially when the size and diversity of the relevant public greatly exceeds the optimum level for direct engagement in deliberative processes. There is the question of how to represent the interests of future generations fairly when present generations are particularly vocal. The question of how to best address technological complexity and knowledge limitations when engaging the general public in deliberative processes can be a thorny one. And time constraints or urgency may preclude use of deliberation at all.

The challenges of managing multi-stakeholder deliberation reinforce the need for building capacity, managing expectations and ensuring sufficient resource inputs for the process. The successes of watershed management councils in Australia and Oregon, for example, have raised expectations for multi-stakeholder deliberative mechanisms for natural resources management, without concomitant recognition of the need for resources to support these efforts (Curtis et al., 2002).

LINKS TO OTHER ADAPTIVE POLICY TOOLS

Deliberative approaches can be combined with most of the other adaptive policy tools we identify. Integrated and forward-looking analysis (Chapter 3) can support deliberative approaches by providing participants in the process with analytical conclusions useful in assessing options and making choices. This was the approach taken in the case of zero-tillage cultivation methods in Saskatchewan, for example, where researchers and farm groups analyzed options and shared their conclusions as part of the deliberative process that led to farmers adopting the system very rapidly. And as discussed earlier, deliberative processes can support integrated and forward-looking analysis by providing the multiple perspectives necessary to understand complex issues.

Formal policy review and continuous improvement mechanisms (Chapter 9) are also often built into policies designed as the result of deliberative processes, in part because of the high public profile and concern engendered by such processes. Because deliberative mechanisms can build social capital and strengthen local institutions, they are often used as part of a strategy to identify and encourage self-organization and social networks (Chapter 6), such as in the case of farmer-to-farmer extension networks for zero-tillage in Saskatchewan.

Table 4.1 Overview of Multi-stakeholder Deliberation

Multi-stakeholder deliberation: Multi-stakeholder deliberation is a collective and collaborative public effort to examine an issue from different points of view in order to share learning and build consensus about the appropriate course of action, prior to taking a decision. Deliberative processes strengthen policy design by building recognition of common values, shared commitment and emerging issues, and by providing a comprehensive understanding of causal relationships.

Why?	What is it?	How to apply it?	When to use it?
• To deal with the unexpected trajectories of preference, priorities and social response to changes. • To provide access to innovative perspectives. • Ecosystem boundaries do not conform to a single sector. • Public discourse and open deliberation are important elements of social learning and policy adaptation (Stone, 2001; Roberts, 2004). • To build trust, collaboration, consensus, identity, values, hope and capacity for social action (Forester, 1999).	• Participation is voluntary. • The effort is structured and led by skilled facilitators. • The process accommodates and respects, even values, plural perspectives. • While deliberative processes are not generally designed to negotiate conflicts, they should be able to handle conflicting views and negotiation of common interests. • Participants should include a broad range of stakeholders directly or indirectly affected by the decision. • Deliberative proceedings are transparent and accessible. • Deliberation is aimed at an explicit decision context.	*Preparation* • Basic procedural issues (for example, facilitation, decision-making) need to be clarified by organizers. • Face-to-face deliberation is most effective. *Participant Selection* • Engage marginal groups to balance power differentials. • Involve stakeholders from the beginning. *Deliberation* • Build communication competencies (for example, listening, non-threatening questioning). • Leadership is vital—participants take cues from those who model reflective, respectful and open language. • Participants should ideally be engaged in doing, not just listening.	• For understanding and framing issues and in setting objectives. • For evaluation, learning and adaptation stages of policy implementation. • In situations where decisions are contentious and stakeholders are vocal or well organized. • Used in response to situations where there is dissatisfaction with current decision-making. • Should only be used if it can be seen to be equitable, accessible and enabling social learning. If it is manipulative, or purely symbolic, the process is likely to generate even greater resentment and polarization. • Not a model for simple problem solving.

But perhaps the most obvious linkage between deliberative mechanisms and other adaptive policy tools is in the case of decentralization (Chapter 7), where the devolution of decision-making on resource management issues usually complements the adoption of deliberative practices at the local level. The cases of Manitoba CDs, southern Alberta Irrigation Districts and Maharashtra watershed management all point to examples of this phenomenon. By strengthening local deliberative processes, the devolution of decision-making authority is more likely to achieve the intended results.

5   Automatic Policy Adjustment

Suruchi Bhadwal, Stephan Barg
and Darren Swanson

> **What is automatic policy adjustment?** Some of the
> inherent variability in socio-economic and ecologic
> conditions under which a policy must operate can be
> anticipated, and monitoring can help trigger import-
> ant policy adjustments to keep the policy functioning
> well.

WHY IS AUTOMATIC ADJUSTMENT IMPORTANT FOR CREATING ADAPTIVE POLICIES?

Changes in economic, social and environmental conditions are normal. In
Chapters 3 and 4 we emphasized that understanding a policy from multiple
perspectives, both analytically and through deliberative processes with
stakeholders and experts, can help policy-makers anticipate future conditions
under which the policy will need to operate. Armed with this understanding
policy-makers can perform two functions. The first function was introduced in
Chapter 3 and involves identifying a specific policy or a feature of a policy that
enables it to perform successfully under a range of plausible future conditions,
and possibly even under a worst case scenario.

Consider an example of hydropower development in the face of increasing
drought potential caused by climate change. A risk management strategy in
such a case might be to diversify the power supply by developing a source that
is uncorrelated with the drought risk. Development of wind power could be
a robust policy under such anticipated future conditions. It is an example of
something that can be done now that would help the power supply system
perform successfully in a range of anticipated future climatic conditions. If
costs are similar to hydropower, and the socio-economic and environmental
impacts are less than or similar to the existing sources, then this can be considered a no-regrets type of policy for the future.

But it is certainly not always the case that a no-regrets type of policy or policy feature can be identified in advance. It is quite likely however that, given information from integrated assessment (Chapter 3) and deliberation (Chapter 4), a policy-maker will be able to anticipate a future socio-economic or environmental change that would affect the performance of the policy. With this anticipation it is possible to identify in advance how the policy would need to be adjusted to maintain performance. This function involves pre-defining the policy adjustment, monitoring the changes in socio-economic and environmental conditions, and triggering the policy adjustment at the appropriate time. Of course there will be differing degrees to which the policy adjustment can be pre-defined, and this will be discussed later in this chapter.

This second functionality, to adjust policy over time, helps accomplish in part an important element of adaptive assessment and management that Holling (1978) advocated: that monitoring and remedial mechanisms be integral to policy design, and not be *ad hoc* additions after implementation. This function also speaks to experiences in policy-making for improving healthcare in cities. Glouberman et al. (2003) recognized that 'in complex systems, which change over time and respond dynamically to outside forces, it is necessary to constantly refine interventions'. Experience with transportation policy also points to the need for ongoing policy adjustment. Walker and Marchau (2003), in recommending a policy process for considering airport expansion alternatives in the Netherlands, recommended that 'learning and adaptation of the policy be made explicit at the outset and the inevitable policy changes become part of a larger, recognized process and are not forced to be made repeatedly on an ad hoc basis'.

WHAT IS AUTOMATIC ADJUSTMENT?

Automatic policy adjustment mechanisms help policies respond well in variety of plausible and clearly identified future circumstances. They can speed up the process of response to conditions that are more or less anticipated. They can be used in complicated policy environments by separating the various policy issues into units wherein the understanding of the system is high, allowing for fine-tuning of the system and making adjustments that help reduce risks and maintain performance.

Automatic adjustment can be both *fully-* and *semi-automatic*. *Fully-automatic* adjustment can be used in a policy if the conditions that trigger the adjustment and the policy adjustment itself can be pre-defined. *Semi-automatic* policy adjustment is similar to fully-automatic adjustment in that it requires pre-definition of the triggering conditions, but the precise adjustment cannot be designed in advance. Some additional analysis and deliberation is necessary. These differences between *fully-automatic* and *semi-automatic* policy adjustment begins to define a continuum for how policy can be improved based on new information (Figure 5.1). Further along the spectrum are cases where systems are comparatively less predictable and policy adjustments are manual, requiring a process of analysis and deliberation to review the policy, learn why it is not meeting its goals and to design the necessary improvement in the policy. A fully manual policy adjustment approach deals primarily with unanticipated conditions and is discussed in Chapter 9 on formal policy review and continuous learning.

Figure 5.1   Spectrum of Policy Adjustment

Anticipated Conditions (system well understood)	Anticipated Conditions (system not so well understood, but can be better understood over time)	Unanticipated Conditions (system not so well understood)
Fully-automatic policy adjustment	*Semi-automatic policy adjustment*	*Formal policy review and continuous learning*

Examples of Fully-automatic Policy Adjustment

We observed several examples of fully-automatic policy adjustment in our research in Canada and India. Weather-indexed insurance in India is a particularly good example. It has emerged as an alternative to traditional crop insurance in India where settling a claim was a time-consuming process. Weather-indexed crop insurance is linked to the underlying weather risk measured by an index based on historical climate data, rather than the extent of crop yield loss. These weather insurance contracts have been found to offer quick payouts triggered by independently monitored weather indices and result in improved recovery times from weather-related stress. The automatic adjustment feature provides a simple mechanism for managing insurer risk and determining farmer eligibility for benefit payments, while passing along incentives to farmers to adjust to long-term change by providing appropriate signals calculated on the basis of actuarial risks (Kelkar, 2006).

Two additional examples, also related to crop insurance, were seen in the Canadian province of Manitoba. These include the Pasture Drought Insurance Pilot Program and the Fall Frost Insurance Pilot Program which were introduced in 2007. The Pasture Drought Insurance Pilot Program is designed 'to evaluate the need for a weather derivative type insurance program that compensates producers for losses to pasture production due to lack of rainfall as recorded at a specified weather station' (MASC, 2007a). Producers participating in this pilot programme do not need to submit a claim nor do they require an on-farm inspection of their pasture. This weather-triggered insurance programme assigns an Environment Canada weather station to the producer's land and a claim is 'triggered when their assigned weather station reports that rainfall within the area fell below 80% of normal'. The Fall Frost Insurance Pilot Program is designed in a similar fashion (MASC, 2007b).

The concept of automatic adjustment appears to be internalized in the crop insurance arena, going as far back as the early days of crop insurance. An excerpt from a 1940 report of the Province of Manitoba's Economic Survey Board illustrates this early adoption:

> ... there is evidence that in some counties, the level of insurance was somewhat too high. This has pointed to the need for an automatic control which has been incorporated into the 1940 program. Under this method, if the aggregate of individual insured yields and premium rates is out of line with the county actuarial data, a factor is applied to adjust them to the proper level.
>
> Economic Survey Board (1940: 10)

'Automatic stabilizers' are another example of fully-automatic policy adjustment. These are expenditure instruments that operate on the opposite cycle to the economy as a whole: when the economy is growing, automatic stabilizers spend less money, and when the economy is shrinking, they spend more. The net result is that the expenditures take place at a time when they will help the economy out of a downturn. One standard example is unemployment insurance, which pays out to people who become unemployed. In a paper reviewing Canada's Unemployment Insurance (UI) system, Dungan and Murphy (1995) found that the UI policy instrument had a clear stabilizing effect on the Canadian economy. They note that '...it takes time before the problem of rising unemployment or a sluggish economy is recognized'. Because there is a further lapse of time before policy decisions are made, implemented and have an effect on the economy, economists and policy-makers look for 'automatic stabilizers' that respond immediately when the economy slips from the level of full employment. Such automatic stabilizers should respond quickly—changing taxes, or increasing or reducing government spending—to even out the economic impacts of cyclical fluctuations. There are two features of the system, now known as Employment Insurance (EI), that make it an automatic stabilizer. First, when unemployment increases, total EI payments increase, with only a short time lag. Second, when people lose their jobs, they and their employers immediately stop paying the EI premiums associated with those jobs. When an economic downturn results in fewer jobs, the total tax represented in EI premiums immediately falls. At the same time, increased payments in EI benefits put some purchasing power back into the economy by automatically increasing government spending.

Examples of Semi-automatic Policy Adjustment

All of these examples of fully-automatic policy adjustment described in the foregoing are used in conditions that are more or less anticipated in nature and are based on triggers and policy adjustments that can be pre-defined. But this level of information is not always available. In many situations, the precise policy adjustment requires some further assessment and deliberation, such as that described in Chapters 3 and 4. We refer to this form of policy adjustment as semi-automatic.

An example of semi-automatic policy adjustment was observed in Canada's Western Grain Transportation Act (WGTA). The freight rate for transporting grain across the Canadian Prairies was originally a fixed rate under the WGTA's predecessor, the Crow Rate. As summarized in Chapter 3, this fixed rate survived the better part of a century and had a disastrous impact on the upkeep of the rail transportation system. Under the new WGTA a variable transportation rate calculation was introduced, based on the railways' 'cost of moving grain and intended to cover variable costs plus 20% toward constant costs'. This cost was based on forecasts of grain volumes by the Grain Transportation Agency and on railway costs provided by the National Transportation Agency. The rate was also distance-based, designed to allow equal rates for equal distances (Producer Payment Panel, 1994).

Another example of semi-automatic policy adjustment is the Canada Pension Plan (CPP) to account for adequate retirement income in the face of an aging population and economic change. A regular review process has been set to examine whether changes are required in the CPP to reflect the growing pensionable population still part of the labour force (Government of Canada, 2006). If the payments into the fund are insufficient to pay the pensions, the rates or coverage levels will need to be changed. The US Social Security

Program through the Social Security Amendments of 1983 sought to keep the programme solvent for the next 75 years, that is, until 2058. A review of the programme basically indicated a future shortfall requiring *ad hoc* changes that are rather untimely or establishing a mechanism to automatically adjust the programme back into balance.

Situations where unanticipated events impinge on policy performance are not handled well by the automatic adjustment approach, be it fully- or semi-automatic. In such unanticipated conditions, more careful formal review is required to assess the need for adjustment and to define the precise nature of the adjustment. This is the focus of Chapter 9.

HOW TO USE AUTOMATIC POLICY ADJUSTMENT

In order to use the automatic adjustment mechanism, several issues arise, namely the definition of the policy issue, and an understanding of the limits within which the policy can be expected to operate well. The first is important in designing exactly what the automatic adjustment should be—in the case of the Employment Insurance system, the rules about premium and payment rates. Tools, like integrated and forward-looking analysis (Chapter 3) and multi-stakeholder deliberation (Chapter 4), can help ensure that the system is well understood. Understanding the limits within which the policy can be expected to operate is important in designing a monitoring system for the ongoing policy in order to measure its success and also to establish signposts and triggers to help with ongoing policy review and evolution.

As introduced in Chapters 2 and 3, Walker et al. (2001) provide lucid guidance and a working vocabulary for policy adjustment in their account of adaptive policy-making in the transportation sector. With clear policy objectives set, options identified and successful performance defined, the researchers recommend developing indicators or *signposts* as they refer to it, to track critical information to determine whether policy adjustment or reassessment is required. For each signpost a trigger is identified—a critical value of the signpost indicator that leads to implementation of certain actions. These actions (that is, adjustments) are further categorized as either *corrective actions* (to adjust the basic policy) or *defensive action* (taken after the fact to preserve a policy's benefits). The researchers use the example of expansion policy for Amsterdam Airport Schiphol in the Netherlands as an illustration. In this context, a signpost might include the growth of air transport demand with the trigger being slower than expected growth and the corrective action being a delay in the expansion of the airport. The economic viability of the anchor airline, KLM, could be another signpost, with the trigger being an early warning of financial insolvency and defensive actions being to support the airline, reduce competition from other airlines or attract another anchor airline for the airport.

Some of these examples of signposts, triggers and *fully-automatic* policy adjustments are summarized in Table 5.1.

Walker et al. (2001) also describe that many policy adjustments can also be handled at the discretion of the policy implementers—who can decide, based on the policy objectives, to defend the policy as it is, or pursue the objective by other means. In this guidebook we refer to this as semi-automatic policy adjustment. In situations where neither corrective or defensive actions are enough to ensure policy objectives are met, because of the unanticipated actions of others or large shocks to signposts, Walker et al. (2001) recommend a complete policy reassessment. This latter action we elaborate on in Chapter 9 on formal policy review and continuous learning in the context of unanticipated conditions.

In order to use the fully-automatic or semi-automatic adjustment instrument, the policy designer would first examine the policy situation that is faced for well-understood and anticipated future events. With this analysis, the designer would develop a set of signposts and triggers which could be written into the enabling legislation or other policy instrument that implements the policy. An overview of automatic policy adjustments as an adaptive policy-making tool is provided in Table 5.2.

WHEN TO USE AUTOMATIC ADJUSTMENT

Before discussing more specifically when automatic adjustment is used in the policy design and implementation cycle, we first clarify when not to use this mechanism. When an integrated and forward-looking analysis (Chapter 3) and multi-stakeholder deliberation (Chapter 4) leave questions as to how the policy would be designed in various potential future circumstances, it is an indication that the automatic adjustment mechanism may not be the tool to use. Automatic adjustment requires that there is sufficient understanding of anticipated conditions under which the policy will function, and that policy adjustments can be clearly defined in response to the anticipated conditions.

But as illustrated in the previous section, signpost indicators can indeed be developed in many circumstances and fully-automatic policy adjustments can be pre-defined or made at the discretion of policy implementers and designers (semi-automatic adjustment). In the case of fully-automatic adjustment,

Table 5.1 Examples of Signposts, Triggers and Policy Adjustments

Policy	Signpost	Trigger	Adjustment
Drought—pasture insurance (Manitoba)	Rainfall at specified government weather station	When rainfall for the applicable weather station falls below 80 per cent of normal during the growing season (April, May, June and July). Actual rainfall, as a percentage of normal, is calculated on a month-by-month basis and is capped at a maximum of 150 per cent of normal. A weighting is given to each month: 10 per cent for April; 40 per cent for May; 40 per cent for June; and 10 per cent for July (MASC, 2007a).	For every percentage point that the current year's rainfall falls below 80 per cent of normal, the producer is given double the loss. For example, if rainfall for a given area is 60 per cent of normal, a producer in this area would receive (80–60 per cent) × 2 = 40 per cent loss (MASC, 2007a).
Fall—frost insurance (Manitoba)	Temperature at specified government weather station	When a temperature of −2° Celsius or lower is recorded at the local Environment Canada weather station for 14 or more days prior to the normal fall frost date (MASC, 2007b).	Coverage of $15 per acre on most insured crops (MASC, 2007b).
Employment Insurance (EI) (Canada)	Unemployment rate	Increasing unemployment rate.	Total EI payments increase, with only a short time lag.
		Decreasing unemployment rate.	Total tax represented in EI premiums immediately falls.
		Employee loses job.	At the same time, increased payments in EI benefits put some purchasing power back into the economy by automatically increasing government spending.
			Employee and employer immediately stop paying the EI premiums associated with those jobs.

Table 5.2 Overview of Automatic Adjustment

Automatic policy adjustment: Some of the inherent variability in socio-economic and ecologic conditions under which a policy must operate can be anticipated, and monitoring can help trigger important policy adjustments to keep the policy functioning well.

Why?	What is it?	How to apply it?	When to use it?
• Changes in economic, social and environmental conditions are normal, and it is not always possible to design a policy that is robust to all anticipated conditions. • Monitoring and remedial mechanisms should be integral to policy design, and not be *ad hoc* additions after implementation (Holling, 1978). • In complex adaptive systems, which change over time and respond dynamically to outside forces, it is necessary to constantly refine interventions (Glouberman et al., 2003).	**Fully-automatic adjustment:** • Where a thorough understanding of the policy issue can articulate anticipated changes in underlying conditions, and allows for a specific policy adjustment to be pre-defined. **Semi-automatic adjustment** • Where a thorough understanding of the policy issue can articulate anticipated changes in underlying conditions, but for which specific policy adjustments cannot be pre-defined.	Integrated and forward-looking analysis (Chapter 3) and multi-stakeholder deliberation (Chapter 4) can be used to develop the following components (from Walker et al, 2001): • *Signposts*—critical information to monitor so as to determine whether policy adjustment or reassessment is required. • *Triggers*—threshold values of signpost indicators that put in place specific policy adjustments. • *Corrective actions*—to adjust the basic policy. • *Defensive action*—adjustment to preserve a policy's benefits. • *Reassessment*—action taken when unanticipated shocks or actions occur which threaten the validity of the policy (triggers formal review, see Chapter 9).	**Fully-automatic adjustment** • When *policy adjustments* can be pre-defined. • Signposts and triggers, as well as specific adjustments, are developed in the policy design phase. • Adjustments are put in place during policy implementation. **Semi-automatic adjustment** • When *policy adjustments* cannot be pre-defined. • Signposts and triggers are developed in the policy design phase. • Adjustments are crafted and put in place during policy implementation.

the signpost indicators and the specific policy adjustments that are triggered are all developed in the policy design phase. The actual adjustment, however, is of course an action during policy implementation. In the case of semi-automatic adjustment, the signposts and triggers can be defined in the policy design phase, but the actual adjustment is developed and executed during policy implementation.

LINKS TO OTHER ADAPTIVE POLICY TOOLS

The design of an automatic adjustment policy mechanism is predicated on an integrated and forward-looking analysis of the key factors that affect policy performance (Chapter 3) and multi-stakeholder deliberation (Chapter 4). Most specifically, the scenario analysis and planning approach described in Chapter 3 is a practical mode of entry for developing signpost indicators and for providing the necessary information to craft specific policy adjustments, be they fully- or semi-automatic.

The signposts developed for fully- or semi-automatic policy adjustment are also a means for triggering a formal review process (as elaborated on in Chapter 9) for instances where unanticipated severe shocks in signpost indicators are realized or where other underlying socio-economic and environmental conditions emerge that were not foreseen during development of the policy.

6 Enabling Self-organization and Social Networking

Dimple Roy, Sreeja Nair
and Henry David Venema

What is self-organization and social networking?
Ensuring that policies do not undermine existing social
capital; creating forums that enable social networking;
facilitating the sharing of good practices; and removing
barriers to self-organization, all strengthen the ability
of stakeholders to respond to unanticipated events in
a variety of innovative ways.

WHY IS ENABLING SELF-ORGANIZATION AND SOCIAL NETWORKING IMPORTANT FOR ADAPTIVE POLICIES?

The capacity of individuals and groups to self-organize around problems, stresses and crises has been well recorded in social and biological literature and keenly affects the ability of communities to adapt to changing circumstances. The relationship between social networks and resilience has also been highlighted in many contexts, including that of climate change impacts and responses. A well-known example to demonstrate the link would be that of the New Orleans flood in the United States in 2005. The day the floods began to hit the community the hardest, locals remember there being no one around to help—the fire department was overwhelmed, much of the police force had left and government representatives were in short supply. The army of volunteers that appeared in the middle of this chaos was attributed by Lejano and Ingram (2008) to social networking. These volunteers, dressed in yellow T-shirts, carried vast amounts of emergency supplies and came from the Mormon Church. They displayed a strong sense of organization where other formal programmes had failed. The authors use this as an example of the ability of an ongoing social network to respond to unexpected circumstances. The success of this social networking is attributed to the fact that it existed before the breakdown of formal relief systems, and allowed those within this network to communicate even when formal lines of communication (including phone lines) failed.

In a similar example, when an earthquake measuring 8.0 on the Richter scale hit Sichuan province in China on 12 May 2008, thousands died in the country. The earthquake was followed by two aftershocks and caused extensive destruction. While the situation made it difficult to focus on the positive, the response efforts included something that had not been seen commonly in similar situations of crisis in China —the ability of people to self-organize and help each other out. The *Globe and Mail*, a Canadian newspaper, described it as 'extraordinary' and explained that much of the response was improvised and instinctive, yet it meshed together in unexpectedly efficient ways, using the best of government muscle, military power, corporate resources, individual volunteerism and grassroots creativity. There was no sign of looting or violence in the disaster zone, despite all the pressures on the survivors (as seen in similar contexts in the past). This example demonstrates the ability of 'informal' networks and social groups to deal with crisis even in ways complementary to official relief and rehabilitation.

An important demonstration of the value of self-organization and social networks emerged from our case study on Irrigation Districts (IDs) in Alberta, Canada. An ID is a corporation that is responsible for the delivery of irrigation water to farmers and for the maintenance of irrigation infrastructure. Each ID operates independently based on its size and unique physical characteristics. In response to a severe drought in 2001, pre-existing IDs convened a multi-agency coordinating committee to construct and implement a mitigation and preparedness plan in case the conditions did not improve by the start of the 2001 irrigation season (Swanson et al., 2008). The programme in the St. Mary River Irrigation District (SMRID) was instrumental in developing networks in the region to work together to construct emergency preparedness plans.

Self-organization was also facilitated through the introduction of formal and informal markets within the IDs in Alberta. In the SMRID, water rationing from the 2001 shortages precipitated the creation of an informal market for trading water allocations. Nichol (2005) found that the majority of buyers and sellers found each other through word of mouth, though some buyers found sellers hard to locate. The SMRID now maintains a list of potential buyers and sellers on its website.

These examples demonstrate the importance of the inherent capacity of people to 'self-organize' in times of crisis and to develop solutions in the absence of formal direction. This inherent capacity can be built and harnessed through adaptive policy development as a powerful tool to help deal with 'unanticipated' change in the future.

Glouberman et al. (2003), in developing a toolbox for improving health in cities, recognized that complex adaptive systems 'often spontaneously generate solutions to problems without external input or formally organized interventions. This self-organizing capacity is a free good that can be valuable in producing innovative and novel approaches to problems'. Gunderson et al. (1995) clarify that ecosystem responses to resource use and the reciprocal response of people to changes in ecosystems constitute coupled, dynamic systems that exhibit adaptive behaviour. Berkes et al. (2003) cite this charac-teristic of adaptive systems as synonymous with ecological, economic and social sustainability and one that exhibits multiple states of equilibrium. According to them, in the absence of a linear, mechanical universe that would have permitted simple, rational measures, the best bet for sustainability involves the capability for self-organization in socio-ecological systems.

WHAT IS SELF-ORGANIZATION AND SOCIAL NETWORKING?

Self-organizing has been described as the process of social interaction around common issues that, from a policy perspective, enables the group to identify and implement innovative solutions. This process of self-organizing has been described as *social networking, building social capital, participation* and *collaboration*. The intent of this chapter is to tease out aspects of the process of self-organizing and social networking to ascertain the important enablers and clarify how self-organization leads to policy solutions that will adapt well to unforeseen circumstances.

Social networks are defined by Lejano and Ingram (2008) as a system of sustained, patterned relationships among actors, which cross and sometimes blur organizational boundaries. They further say that social networks can be a part of a formal institution, purely informal or even purely social. Such networks may be driven by function, but this is not the essence of the network—what characterizes it is the system of lasting relationships. Social networks allow the ability to pool knowledge and concerns and are the mechanism by which adaptability and resilience are built into an institution through variation of responses and multi-stakeholder deliberation discussed in Chapters 8 and 4 respectively. This, in turn, allows the programme to survive system changes and find new innovative practices.

It is important here to differentiate between organization (that is, mandated networks for problem-solving and implementation) and self-organization (that is, the ability of people to build networks *themselves* to better deal with an issue). This chapter deals with the latter, while Chapter 7 (Decentralization of Decision-making) addresses the former. While the capacity of the groups mentioned in the New Orleans, China and Alberta Irrigation District examples was facilitated by their existing membership in a formal organization, the groups had re-organized themselves around issues that were not mandated by any higher authority. The value of a common forum to enable people to self-organize is discussed later in this chapter.

Research suggests that policy should not directly seek to mandate *self-organization* through building social capital and, in fact, explicitly promoting it might have negative outcomes. The Policy Research Initiative (PRI, 2005) indicates that their research has yielded repeated warnings that public policy-makers should be very careful in choosing to explicitly target social capital investment for policy purposes. Some representatives from community organizations expressed a degree of wariness towards government efforts to tap local social resources lest they become substitutes for tangible government assistance. Perri (1997) has cautioned that there have been few robust evaluations of the efficacy of those interventions deliberately designed to shape social capital formation. Moreover, he noted that promoting one type of social capital (such as bridging ties between disparate communities) to achieve one set of policy objectives may have the unintended consequence of undermining other patterns of social capital (such as strong bonding ties within communities) that are required to achieve other policy goals.

Policies may instead focus on removing the barriers that would prevent people from self-organizing around an unanticipated situation when it arises. These barriers could be physical, financial, social, informational or other resource barriers.

Social capital is generally defined as the relationships, networks and norms that facilitate collective action (Helliwell, 2001). Social capital refers to features of social organization, such as networks, norms and trust that facilitate coordination and cooperation for mutual benefit. The central idea of social capital, according to Putnam (2001), includes networks and the associated norms of reciprocity. The Government of Canada's PRI (2005) elaborated on the direct and indirect ways of influencing social capital by explicitly building supporting networks to implicitly incorporate increased programme sensitivity to existing social capital in policy. This continuum from indirect to direct programming is demonstrated in Figure 6.1.

Figure 6.1   Making Use of Social Capital in Public Policy: From Direct to Indirect Influence

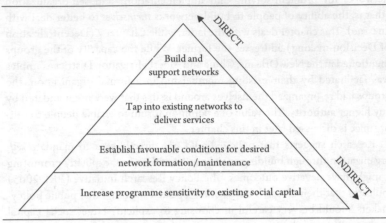

Source: PRI (2005).

Examples of self-organization abound in natural resources management literature. Lise (2000) documents a forest site in Uttar Pradesh in India where forest councils have long existed. People demanded the right to self-organize, with formal rights for the communal management of forest resources. Forest councils consist of villagers and the role of the state in management is minimal. Coastal systems have also been found at times to self-organize in this fashion (Ruitenbeek and Cartier, 2001). Sathirathai (1998) documents the self-organization of coastal communities in Thailand when their mangrove resources fell into steep decline, and central government subsequently stepped in to give further assistance. An overview of self-organization and social networking as a tool for policy-making is provided in Table 6.1.

HOW TO APPLY SELF-ORGANIZATION AND SOCIAL NETWORKS IN ADAPTIVE POLICY-MAKING

A primary pre-condition that influences the capacity of people to self-organize is the existence of adequate social capital. While many definitions and explanations exist for the concept of social capital, it simply refers to the networks of social relations that may provide individuals and groups with access to resources and supports (PRI, 2005). While social capital is difficult to measure, a healthy community or group with adequate social capital is discernable and valuable as a means to deal with uncertainty. While self-organization is usually recorded as people's response to crisis, or a lack of policy in a certain area, the capacity to self-organize can be built and enhanced to respond to unanticipated events.

The notion of the development of social networks self-organizing around common issues is highlighted by Lejano and Ingram (2008). These collaborations are often place-bound, implying that commonality between the members is important (of time, place, condition, joy and suffering). This means that these groups are not just communicating, they are experiencing stresses together. This is an important impetus for self-organization in itself.

For effective intervention in complex adaptive systems, leveraging the self-organizing potential of people to address an issue is perhaps one of the most commonly cited principles. Lejano and Ingram (2008) explain that social networks can be activated when needed, can be perturbed for new information or ways of doing things, or simply turned to as an extensive store of knowledge. For the purpose of determining the sorts of policy interventions that can help self-organization, we looked towards the social capital literature and policy interventions that have been cited in literature to strengthen social capital. Van Kemenade et al. (2003) describe social capital as primarily involving social networks, civic engagement and confidence and having a direct influence on the way people work together.

Lejano and Ingram (2008) explain three useful concepts for understanding how interaction works: proximity, activation and space. These concepts can be used to harness complexity by altering patterns of interaction.

- *Proximity* factors determine how agents within a system (or people within a social setting) will be likely to interact with each other.
- *Activation* factors determine the sequencing of their activity.
- *Space* encompasses the concept of proximity, and includes physical and conceptual space (such as hierarchy in an organization) to promote interaction.

These factors allow us to analyze the basis of social interaction and resulting self-organization from a causal point of view and provide insights into potential policy interventions to enhance such social networks. Giving us similar direction in removing barriers to social interaction and self-organization, Margerum (2007) describes constraints to local collaboration as transaction costs, limited perspectives, organizational sustainability, policy issues and adequacy of representation. There is some indication in literature that social capital and the ability of people to self-organize can be enhanced, but not too explicitly. The notion of adaptive policies as policies that promote self-organization and social networks might prove more effective if they focused on removing the barriers to self-organization instead.

While the value of such social networks and self-organization is espoused in a wide range of literature, our primary interest lies in policy tools that will enable us to enhance such self-organization potential to create resilience and deal better with known and unknown stresses. Our search for supportive policy mechanisms has revealed the following key characteristics for policies to directly or indirectly enhance and enable self-organization and social networks as a positive mechanism to cope with uncertainty:

- Ensure that social capital remains intact (Ruitenbeek and Cartier, 2001).
- Create and promote effective spaces and issues for adaptive cooperation (Axelrod and Cohen, 2000).
- Facilitate copying through promotion of best practices and enhance leadership (ibid.).
- Remove resource barriers to self-organization (Koontz, 2006).

Ensure that Social Capital Remains Intact

As in most conservation practice, where the first rule of intervention is to 'do no harm', a comparative principle in enhancing social interaction and encouraging self-organization is to ensure that existing social capital remains intact. Ruitenbeek and Cartier (2001) suggest that foremost for intervention in complex adaptive systems, policies must *ensure that social capital remains intact.* If local groups and their networks are disempowered individually or collect-ively, existing social structures are in effect invalidated and undermined. PRI (2005) echoes this notion in their report on social capital as a public policy tool, where they state that the first rationale for an explicit incorporation of social capital into policies and programmes is to avoid inadvertent harm to useful existing sources of social capital. This means that in undertaking integrated and forward-looking analysis (see Chapter 3) during policy design, social networks ought to be considered a part of design parameters. Questions such as 'What sort of networks exist in the policy context?' 'How can volunteers or local networks that already address the policy issue be enhanced?' and 'What motivations for social networking can be built into the policy design?' may be included in the policy analysis during design and implementation.

In the context of a watershed-based volunteer group programme in Victoria, Australia, Curtis et al. (2002) highlight that understanding volunteer motivation is fundamental to sustaining broad stakeholder participation.

Volunteer literature describes social interaction as the most important factor in retaining its members. They have also established group protocols and norms that encourage broad stakeholder representation. Other motivations include the desire to work locally on national issues; to effect improvement in environmental conditions through on-ground work, for the benefit of social interaction; and to learn about land and water management (Curtis and Van Nouhuys, 1999).

Create and Promote Effective Issue-based Spaces for Adaptive Cooperation

Axelrod and Cohen (2000) stress 'proximity' as a driver for 'interaction', a concept akin to social networking. Promotion of such effective neighbourhoods for adaptive cooperation could involve enabling community programmes, or making community funding available to allow for a group to interact and determine the best use for the resources. Simply defining a community—such as in the case of clearly defined sub-watersheds—may enable the formation of groups that work in the interest of the local watershed.

A substantial section of the debate highlights the role of 'stress' or 'crisis' as a motivation for communities or groups of people to gather around. While it may not be in the best interest of policy to recreate stress to enable self-organization, it might be possible to identify issue-based spaces around which people might collaborate.

Substantiating this point, Koontz (2006) stresses the value of issue and scale identification for effective collaboration. He describes the case of collaborative environmental management in Ohio that was induced in part by the Ohio Farmland Preservation Planning Program that defined clear objectives centreing in preserving farmland and creating a fairly narrow 'space' around which local people could focus. In addition, the programme bound grant-giving to a bio-physical space—the county—and this further allowed self-organization in the physical and issue space. The author stresses the appropriateness of the physical scale chosen for the programme and the importance of scale in contributing to social self-organization. Not only are the counties the same unit at which data for soil types are available in Ohio, the counties are small enough to make task-force meetings accessible to any county resident. Forest councils in India described earlier in this chapter (Lise, 2000) follow this same principle of space-bound issues. In cases where policies may be bound spatially or by local issues, policy design may incorporate outreach and implementation to encourage local stakeholders to create their own networks and implementation groups.

This factor of 'issue identification' as a driver of social network development is highlighted in our community case study on the Saskatchewan Soil Conservation Association (SSCA). The formation of the SSCA was itself a demonstration of the ability of people in Saskatchewan, Canada, to self-organize around a priority of soil conservation after droughts in the 1970s and 1980s. Government policy harnessed this ability of people to self-organize around this issue by funding the creation of a grassroots organization to take up this issue. A group of farmers helped by federal government funding and aided by academic researchers and agri-industry proponents of conservation tillage and related technical inputs, 'self-organized' around this issue and promoted the practice of conservation tillage in a variety of ways. This ability of farmers to self-organize has allowed them to adapt their practices to incorporate current challenges of carbon sequestration through conservation tillage as a means of mitigating climate change and diversifying farm income.

Some authors, such as O'Toole and Burdess (2004), have shown the value of stress in creating social networks. In their account of community governance in Victoria, Australia, they describe the self-organization that resulted from a vacuum in local government due to the amalgamation of municipalities. The authors describe these self-organized community groups that are all involved in some form of self-governing for the collective benefit of the community. In one way or the other, these groups have all attempted to replace a governance vacuum left by the removal of their previous local government authorities. While the groups were originally created to fill perceived gaps, authors also note that membership in these community groups ebb and flow, but 'during special circumstances such as crisis meetings, the attendance will increase dramatically'. Such crisis-based social networking may provide useful lessons during subsequent policy design to address the issues related to the crisis. For example, the New Orleans example described earlier may act as a lesson for any disaster preparedness policies that may emerge for subsequent natural disasters in the region.

Facilitate Copying through Promotion of Best Practices and Enhance Leadership

In support of facilitating copying, Axelrod and Cohen (2000) identify 'following another agent' as an important enabler of interaction. In our community case study on the SSCA, we noted that the 'farmer-to-farmer' networking programme allowed this sort of 'copying'. Under this programme, farmers who showed interest in conservation tillage practices were put in contact with a farmer in their region who was practising conservation tillage. It was felt that farmers successful with the new and somewhat contentious technique would be the best leaders of change and would be best positioned to influence their peers.

The role of leadership is highlighted in a variety of ways and may be a strong causal factor in translating social capital into social networks. While the role of human resources is important in maintaining social networks, often an entrepreneurial leader must be available to establish a new collaborative group (Moseley, 1999). The role of leadership is best understood through literature from business management models, where effective leadership leads to effective social networking within organizations.

Axelrod and Cohen (2000) also highlight the positive *and negative* aspects of leadership and its role in social networking. One potentially negative aspect of following the leadership of another is simply too much reliance on their interests and ways of achieving goals. Another negative aspect is that other members of the network may not entirely understand the criteria and elements of the combined goal as clearly as the leader and may lead to a less effective form of social capital than a more equitable collective. These might serve as caveats while the effectiveness of leadership is assessed in an adaptive policy context.

Remove Resource Barriers to Self-organization

Collaborative environmental management in Ohio, through the Ohio Farmland Planning Program was initiated in 1996 to encourage counties to gather appropriate data from which local goals could be established relative to the agricultural industry and farmland (Koontz, 2006). Through the state-grant programme, counties received important financial resources in the form of $10,000 awards. Task forces could use the funds to establish groups, provide meeting space and resources, obtain technical information and create plans. The flexibility of the grants allowed each task force to tailor its expenditures to its needs.

Koontz (2006) highlights the value of resources in enabling collaborative environmental management. He divides resources for collaboration into three broad categories: human, technical and financial. While human resources include a collaborative effort's volunteers, leaders and staff members; technical resources refer to knowledge about the environment and about the local context. The financial resources are the funding and in-kind contributions that allow a group to conduct business and perform activities.

In the context of removing constraints to collaboration, Margerum (2007) highlights the need to overcome the transaction costs involved. The author here describes transaction costs as personal time, resources and travel expenses associated with participating in an interactive process. For example, in several large Australian watersheds, community participants had to drive over six hours to attend meetings. Reimbursing travel costs and offering food provided the necessary support for participants to make it to volunteer meetings without sacrificing their needs.

Curtis et al. (2002) demonstrate through the Landcare and Watershed Councils examples in Victoria, Australia, the importance of sustained government funding to overcome resource barriers to self-organization. The authors deliberately challenge the notion that funding programmes that attempt to 'kick-start' a collaborative initiative may not be successful in promoting long-term social interaction. The authors also highlight the need for group coordination, possibly through the resources, by a staff person to manage the social networks and volunteer groups created around the issues of watershed management.

Resources provided to collaborative groups also include information sharing. The role of collective information sharing is highlighted by O'Toole and Burdess (2004) as they describe the community newsletters that play an important role in keeping local communication alive and keeping participants of collaborative efforts informed of the progress being made in local issues and in ensuring that they are able to have their input when necessary. The feeling of common issues and neighbourhood helps in building social capital, a necessary pre-requisite for effective self-organization.

WHEN AND WHERE TO APPLY SELF-ORGANIZATION

In relation to the policy design and implementation cycle described in Chapter 2, self-organization is an innate quality of communities and people that policy-makers must recognize and enhance where possible in the policy design and implementation stages. While it is recognized that self-organization cannot be explicitly mobilized through policy intervention, it can however be enabled indirectly. Ensuring a thorough assessment of existing networks and social interactions at the scenario analysis stage of policy design (Chapter 3), allowing innovative interaction and networking (through provision of a variety of policy instruments [Chapter 8]), and effective multi-stakeholder deliberation (Chapter 4) through policy design and implementation can all help enable self-organization. Along with policy tools prescribing specific actions, tools simply enabling stakeholders to self-organize around potential solutions in innovative ways would be a useful addition to many different kinds of policies.

Social organization can be enabled at the design stage, by simply recognizing the innate tendency of people and groups to self-organize around problems, crises, and articulated issues and spaces. Resources and enabling mechanisms should be allocated at the policy design stage to ensure that social capital is built and that interventions that break down social capital are remedied or terminated. In addition, at the policy implementation stages the methods that have been explained in the foregoing sections may be used: ensuring that social capital is not destroyed; creating and promoting issues and spaces for coordination and communication; enhancing leadership and communicating best practices to enable copying; and removing resource barriers to self-organizing. In addition, the monitoring and evaluation of such inputs to enhance self-organization can be used to determine which interventions actually enhanced social capital and network creation to deal with uncertainty and change.

The innate capacity of people and communities to self-organize is most apparent in the case of crisis, as shown in the New Orleans example at the beginning of this chapter, or in the absence of policy that creates a critical gap in governance, management or administration in a perceivable manner. While this innate ability to manage a situation at the level at which it is most relevant is very useful, it does not lack its share of cynics.

People can self-organize around positive action or get together to destroy infrastructure and promote self-serving causes. The intent of creating social capital in conjunction with sound information and knowledge of sustainable development and the importance of adaptive policies is that any social capital that is created or preserved in this process is used for positive action.

The other challenge with this policy mechanism is its seemingly intangible outcomes and action items. Also, it is almost impossible to actively promote self-organization and its passive nature disallows concrete policy inputs. Unlike the other adaptive policy mechanisms, there is no cause-and-effect analysis that can be applied. While all the positive things to enhance social capital might be planned within a policy, it is possible that one does not see any positive results or outcomes until a time of crisis. And due to its uncertain nature, despite all the inputs, it may not lead to effective action in times of uncertain changes. Challenges to this policy mechanism, therefore, are in its own uncertain nature. The ways to effectively deal with these uncertainty are to provide a sound balance with other relevant mechanisms described in this book: integrated assessment and forward-looking analysis to identify and

Table 6.1 Overview of Enabling Self-organization and Social Networks

Enabling self-organization and social networks: Ensuring that policies do not undermine existing social capital; creating forums that enable social networking; facilitating the sharing of good practices; and removing barriers to self-organization, all strengthen the ability of stakeholders to respond to unanticipated events in a variety of innovative ways.

Why?	What is it?	How to apply it?	When to use it?
• Because policy interventions targeting specific issues cannot always anticipate the necessary responses and mobilize for them. • To leverage the inherent capacity of people to self-organize' around at times of crisis and to develop solutions in the absence of formal direction.	• *Self-organizing* can be described as the process of social interaction around common issues that enables a group to identify and implement innovative solutions. • *Social networks* are a system of sustained, patterned relationships among actors (Lejano and Ingram, 2008) that facilitate the pooling of knowledge, concerns and efforts towards a common cause.	• Ensure that social capital remains intact (Ruitenbeek and Cartier, 2001). • Create and promote effective spaces and issues for adaptive co-operation (Axelrod and Cohen, 2000). • Facilitate copying through promotion of best practices and enhance leadership (ibid.). • Remove resource barriers to self-organization (Koontz, 2006).	• While it is recognized that self-organization cannot be explicitly mobilized through policy intervention, enabling self-organization and social networking is particularly important in mobilizing a variety of innovative responses to unanticipated issues. • Resources and enabling mechanisms should be identified and allocated at the policy design stage. • Self-organization and social networking is an innate quality of communities and people that policy-makers must recognize and enhance where possible in the policy design and implementation stages.

enhance existing social networks and lessons from previous 'crisis-related' self-organization; promoting variation through various instruments that may allow innovative solutions through self-organized networks; and allowing for multi-stakeholder deliberations, where social capital is enhanced and networks are created, are some examples of how self-organization may be enabled using some other, more explicit adaptive policy mechanisms.

LINKS TO OTHER ADAPTIVE POLICY MECHANISMS

Self-organization and social networks are closely linked with a number of the other adaptive policy mechanisms identified and described in this book. A close link to integrated and forward-looking analysis (Chapter 3) is seen in the Saskatchewan case study, where farm groups and industry proponents of conservation tillage explored the various options and shared ideas through a self-organized process enabled by the SSCA.

The most obvious linkages lie with multi-stakeholder deliberation (Chapter 4). Multi-stakeholder deliberation may often be a pre-requisite for self-organization, as seen in the case of community watershed management in Maharashtra and Meghalaya where self-help groups and water-user groups allow people to self-organize around watershed problems (Tomar and Nair, 2008). Like-minded stakeholder groups or communities with common values or ideas around a policy issue are also more likely to self-organize, as in the case of the Mormon Church group in New Orleans described earlier in this chapter.

Another close link lies with the mechanism of variation (Chapter 8), or the notion of a variety of small-scale interventions for the same problem that would enable a range of innovative responses to a problem. We see self-organizational capacity and social networking as a precursor to variation as well as policy variation and innovation potentially leading to self-organization. Allowing people to self-organize and allowing flexibility of thought and action around an identified space or issue may result in a variety of solutions dependent on participants' deliberations.

7 Decentralization of Decision-making

Stephan Barg and Stephen Tyler

What is decentralization of decision-making? Decentralizing the authority and responsibility for decision-making to the lowest effective and accountable unit of governance, whether existing or newly created, can increase the capacity of a policy to perform successfully when confronted with unforeseen events.

WHY IS DECENTRALIZATION IMPORTANT FOR ADAPTIVE POLICIES?

The decentralization of decision-making authority and administrative responsibility to the local level can be an important mechanism in facilitating positive policy responses to unforeseen circumstances. In principle, having decisions made close to the citizens most affected is a way to provide better feedback and ensure that decision-makers are well informed about problems and effects of proposed interventions, as well as the nature of different interests. For policies directly concerning natural resources and ecosystems, decentralization should help decision-makers notice significant change earlier, and mobilize affected local interests to address these changes more simply. The feedback loop between implementation results and policy goals can be effective even though it is informal, which can simplify policy design. Because local conditions and ecosystems vary widely, decentralization provides a way to implement policy more flexibly to ensure effectiveness and adaptation to change.

In studying how to build the resilience of communities for complexity and change in socio-ecologic systems, Berkes et al. (2003) found that it is important to match scales of governance and ecosystems. More specifically, they note that common pool resource users, closely connected to the resource system, are in a better position to adapt to and shape ecosystem change and dynamics than remote levels of governance. Similarly, principles for applying the ecosystem approach for natural resource management highlight the importance for decentralization of decision-making. In 2000, the Conference of the Parties to the United Nations Convention on Biological Diversity endorsed the ecosystem approach and a set of 12 principles (UNEP, 2000). Among these were that 'Management should be decentralized to the lowest appropriate level' (Principle 2) and that 'the ecosystem approach should be undertaken at the appropriate spatial and temporal scales ... that are appropriate to the objectives' (Principle 7). These insights remind us that policy and management efforts must be preceded by a careful determination of the best spatial scale at which to manage and govern a complex issue.

A good example of the usefulness of decentralization can be seen in one of the case studies undertaken for this project, namely that of the Conservation Districts (CDs) in Manitoba, Canada. The CDs were established over a period starting in 1959 and continue in existence. They were tasked with managing soil and water conservation, and given small budgets and access to government staff expertise. They were governed by local boards of directors, but the boards were appointed by the provincial government. Their most interesting successes, from an adaptive policy viewpoint, have been in developing solutions to soil and water management problems that were not foreseen or mentioned in their mandates. This success can be attributed, to a fair degree, to the capacity that the local boards have in making their own decisions as to what issues to tackle and how to deal with them (Barg and Oborne, 2006).

Another case example is that of Water Users Associations (WUAs) in India. These were expressly formed to solicit local input into water use decisions in rural India, where irrigation policy is a critical part of the agricultural economy. Indian water policy is set at the national and state levels and, prior to the introduction of WUAs, was a complex set of policies and institutions that did not allow for substantial local input (Tomar and Nair, 2008).

WHAT IS DECENTRALIZATION OF DECISION-MAKING?

Most public policy is made and delivered in some sort of hierarchy. Many countries have federal systems of government, with a constitutional division of powers into national, state or provincial, and possibly municipal levels. Even in unitary states, there is usually a delegation of government powers to lower administrative levels. *Decentralization* means that decision-making is delegated from units with constitutional authority to units of government lower in the hierarchy. One broad definition is:

> ... the transfer of responsibility for planning, management, and resource-raising and allocation from the central government to *(a)* field units of central government ministries or agencies; *(b)* subordinate units or levels of government; *(c)* semi-autonomous public authorities or corporations; *(d)* area-wide regional or functional authorities; or *(e)* NGOs/PVOs. (Rondinelli, 1981)

A distinction is also typically made between democratic decentralization (sometimes referred to as *devolution*), administrative decentralization (*deconcentration*) and privatization. With regard to *devolution*, responsibilities and authority are transferred to local levels of government. For *deconcentration*, responsibilities are transferred to local field offices of central government agencies, but not to lower levels of government. Privatization is different from both devolution and deconcentration as responsibility is transferred out of government into the private sector (Ribot, 2004). In many cases, decentralization and devolution have been justified by the principle of *subsidiarity*, which has been defined as: 'The principle that tries to ensure that decisions are taken as close as possible to the citizen' (Oxford University Press, n.d.). Subsidiarity is said to improve governance on the grounds, it will strengthen engagement of stakeholders, assessment of consequences and accountability of decision-makers. These factors all contribute to adaptive capacity.

Public policy that aims to affect natural resources will necessarily affect local ecosystems. Therefore, decisions that affect ecosystems need to reflect the knowledge and interests of users or stakeholders of those ecosystems, so that the decisions will be both effective and legitimate. This need for locally oriented decisions may be less salient with respect to economic policy, which tends to have less spatial variation than ecosystems. In terms of the social aspects of decision-making, there may be quite significant variation over short distances in some circumstances and not in others.

There is a tendency for national or state/provincial programmes to be of the 'one-size-fits-all' sort, for reasons of administrative simplicity (Acheson, 2006). Decentralized decision-making allows the decisions to be made at the level where the feedback loops are the tightest, which will allow for quicker and better response to unforeseen circumstances. A decision-making process that takes ecosystem issues into account is most effectively done at the local level, and 'participation by several actors in ecosystem assessments not only broadens the ecosystem assessments, but also improves the legitimacy as well as accuracy of the process' (Fabricius et al., 2007). These factors have a clear bearing on policy adaptability as circumstances change.

The terms 'local' and 'ecosystem' are both unspecific as to precise area, but can be defined so as to fit the systems of focus. For example, the case study on Manitoba CDs dealt with water drainage issues, and the size of the districts approximated that of watersheds. In fact, one of the observations from that case study was that CDs having a boundary aligned with the watershed (rather than municipal boundaries) were more effective at carrying out their mandate (Barg and Oborne, 2006).

Ecosystems are nested in multiple scales, so depending on the management issue in question, the scale of focus will be different. This poses challenges to decentralization of decision-making: some decisions should be decentralized for the reasons outlined earlier, but they will interact with decisions at other scales. Integrated river basin management is a good example, where effective management of the basin as a whole requires devolution of decision-making to smaller sub-basin or local watershed authorities, but requires coordination, policy development and planning to address basin-wide issues (Kemper et al. 2007).

An overview of decentralization as an adaptive policy-making tool is provided in Table 7.1.

HOW TO IMPLEMENT DECENTRALIZED DECISION-MAKING

Decentralization of natural resource management decision-making has been promoted for decades, but it remains difficult to implement. Typically, decentralization faces fierce political opposition from those who stand to lose power or influence. Recent surveys of decentralization experiences in the realm of natural resources and water management from two dozen different countries suggest that the process is fraught with difficulty, yet there are useful lessons for how best to implement decentralization effectively (Kemper et al., 2007; Ribot, 2004). Described in the following is some guidance for effective implementation of decentralization of decision-making, categorized according to aspects of governance, geographic scope, decision-making scope, revenue access and spending capacity, staff and resources, and entrepreneurial capacity.

Governance

Two dimensions of governance are important to successful decentralization. First, the local body responsible for policy implementation and management must be accountable downwards to local stakeholders most directly affected by their decisions. This is fundamental to gaining the benefits of the approach (Ribot, 2004).

In the case of Manitoba CDs, their decision-making boards are selected by elected officials of the rural municipalities within which the district lies and by the provincial government. Proceedings are public and transparent: in some cases hearings on drainage applications are held in the field where the situation can be physically inspected by all concerned. Local government authorities are required to follow high standards of transparency in spending public funds in order to ensure accountability. In addition to this upward accountability, the members of the CD Board are members of the community and are normally responsive to local issues (Barg and Oborne, 2006).

The other important governance dimension of decentralization is the need for appropriate linkages between different levels of government. While decentralization involves delegating authority, there remain several crucial roles for senior governments in resource management: providing technical support, data and analysis; financial assistance; coordination and integration of multi-scale analysis; and legitimate oversight to ensure broad management goals are being met. Such coordination is particularly important in the case of management of watersheds and river basins, where implications of water management and use decisions affect users at multiple scales (Kemper et al., 2007).

Reporting and communicating requirements between levels of government provide the opportunity to learn from adaptive measures and innovations by decentralized authorities. Such actions at the local level will often serve as an early warning for unanticipated issues that will eventually demand a creative central response and will serve as examples for other local bodies confronting similar issues.

These tasks require clear planning, reporting, communicating and oversight linkages between different levels of government. For example, members of Alberta's Irrigation Districts in Canada are irrigation water users. They elect their own board whose deliberations provide a basis for accountability, inclusion, motivation and feedback to policy-makers about the changing interests of irrigation users. These organizations have been called on to make more complex and difficult trade-offs in the face of declining water supply, increased water value, new technologies and pressure to increase deliveries for high-value crops to support local processing industries. Their decisions are subject to allocation decisions being approved by the province through license amendments (Swanson et al., 2008).

In Maharashtra, India, implementation of the National Watershed Development Project for Rainfed Areas (NWDPRA) features decentralized and democratic decision-making which provides more opportunity for local input in watershed management. Special attention is paid to representation of marginal social groups, especially women. In addition, transactions are highly transparent. The roles of players and partners are identified, information exchange is public, there is local accountability for transactions and resources, and there is public accountability to ensure legitimacy.

In Maharashtra, the primary issue is irrigation and maintaining a water supply from groundwater and irrigation systems. The WUAs have a broad mandate to manage irrigation systems, including raising revenue from water charges and allocating water to users (Bhadwal, 2008).

As a programme design issue, the addition of extra layers of decentralization provides more flexibility, but at a cost in design and perhaps operational complexity. The specific aspects to be decentralized will again depend on the issue that the programme is addressing. In the case study of Canada's crop insurance system (Swanson and Venema, 2007), there are three levels of organization. At the national level, programme design, funding, and so on, are dealt with. In each province, detailed rules about coverage are further defined, as well as the province's financial contribution. Finally, district level offices administer much of the actual claim adjustment process. This three-level programme organization fits the needs, whereby there is recognition and funding at the national level regarding risks to farm incomes. But details of the risks to be insured are devolved to provincial decision-making and assessment of claims under the programme are done locally. Water policy in India has similar structures, with a blend of national and state level policy delivered by local level organizations. The Maharashtra Water Users Associations are a good example. As discussed later in this chapter, the policies governing water decision-making in India are a very complex blend of national, state and local legislation and institutions.

However, even a clear statement of the upward accountability of the decentralized authority and its downward responsibility to local stakeholders is not a guarantee of successful adaptive decision-making. Wallington and Lawrence (2007) observe that the example of a newly created layer of local, stakeholder-based units of natural resource management governance in Australia have had limited success in achieving the broad goals the policy change was meant to achieve. Their conclusion is that the social aspects of local decision-making are critical to success and that a shared sense of responsibility among the stakeholders helps make problem-solving work (ibid.).

A further programme design issue is that of coordination among the decentralized bodies. In the case of the Manitoba CDs, there is a branch of the provincial government to which all districts report their financial results, and which has some capacity to direct the District boards. It also provides some central services. This provides the financial and legal oversight called for in the governing legislation. However, there is also an annual meeting of the Conservation Districts Association, which is a voluntary body to which all of the CDs belong. This meeting allows the CDs to exchange best practices and learn from each other, which can enhance the entrepreneurial capacity of the individual CDs. It also provides a feedback mechanism to the government on the overall CD programme, fulfilling an important requirement of adaptive policy.

Geographic Scope

The area to be covered by the decentralized body should relate to the issues it is to address. Both the size and the design of its boundaries will need to be determined. In order to respond to ecosystem management problems, boundaries should reflect the limits of those ecosystems. Of course, ecosystems are also nested and interact at various scales, from the farmer's field to a local landscape, watershed, eco-region and river basin. This reinforces the need for decentralized natural resource management to be designed with linkages and coordination at multiple levels (see the foregoing discussion).

There are thus good arguments both for building decentralized decision-making on existing local government jurisdictions, to take advantage of their accountability mechanisms and overlapping responsibilities; but also for management institutions whose boundaries match the relevant ecological systems. The contradiction between these two approaches can be resolved by designing new institutions at the most appropriate spatial scale, or by adjusting the boundaries of existing local government units, neither of which is a simple or straightforward process.

In case studies of Manitoba CDs and Maharashtra Water Users Associations, the issues relate to water use and drainage for agricultural purposes. In Manitoba, the primary issue is drainage, in the context of broader soil and water management. Many of the CD boundaries were set along the lines of rural municipality boundaries, which do not follow natural, landscape features but rather are straight lines. Following the boundaries of the existing political and management units was convenient, as at the time of formation of the CDs, elected municipal councillors and professional staff played a significant role. Following the existing boundaries recognized the fact that municipalities had significant jurisdiction over policy issues that were important to the CD. For example, road and bridge construction and maintenance are within municipal jurisdiction and are closely related to drainage issues. Some of the drainage canals are also the responsibility of the rural municipalities. In addition to the shared jurisdiction issue, establishing a new set of local CD institutions that consisted of multiple rural municipality members would have been a time-consuming exercise. However, it does seem that the rationale for watershed-based boundaries is strong—some recent boundary changes bring current districts more into line with watershed boundaries and there are frequent calls for reorganizing boundaries along watershed lines (Barg and Oborne, 2006).

In terms of size, the Manitoba CDs range in size from about 700 to approximately 7,000 square kilometres. In a lightly populated countryside, these are not unmanageable sizes. They allow for community input and individual involvement by interested farmers. Alberta Irrigation Districts are relatively smaller and range in size from about 5–1,500 square kilometres (Swanson et al., 2008).

Decision-making Scope

What degree of independence and authority ought to be given to the decentralized body? This is a critical issue, especially in a government setting where legal mandates and authority are key organizational issues. Along with budget and resource issues, the decision-making scope will define the decentralized body's capacity to be innovative and adapt well to unforeseen circumstances. The challenge is to give the body sufficient flexibility of action to have real scope for decision-making and adaptation, but within a framework that sets limits to the mandate. This suggests that the legal mandate of the body should be clear as to goals, and how success is to be measured, but can be expressed broadly enough to allow for flexibility in meeting them (Kemper at al., 2007; Ribot, 2004). Both of the examples listed in the following seem to suggest that the challenges of setting broad goals can be met, even in complex circumstances.

In the case of the CDs in Manitoba, they are given a fair degree of autonomy to undertake things that will further the purposes of the governing legislation, the Conservation Districts Act, which are:

- to provide for the conservation, control and prudent use of resources through the establishment of CDs and
- to protect the correlative rights of owners (Barg and Oborne, 2006).

This definition leaves open wide areas of possible action by the CDs and, as the case study analysis shows, most of their successful adaptive actions were things that were not contemplated when the legislation was passed (Barg and Oborne, 2006). The local boards of directors were able to respond to local needs in new and creative ways. This suggests that the decision-making scope should be kept fairly open, as a way of facilitating the very adaptation that the policy is intended to foster.

In Maharashtra, the development of the WUAs took place in the context of an existing and very complex policy framework for water management. In a drought-prone country, irrigation is a key production strategy and is widely used in India. The administration of irrigation systems, water access and allocation, groundwater usage, and so on, have long been central to agriculture policy, at all levels of government. Beginning in 1987, a greater involvement at the ground level was encouraged to counteract the traditional top-down approach of irrigation administration. The National Water Policy of 1987 called for efforts to 'involve farmers progressively in various aspects of management of irrigation system, particularly in water distribution and collection of water rates' (Tomar and Nair, 2008). In 2005, the Maharashtra Management of Irrigation Systems by Farmers Act was passed, under which WUAs were formed to:

- promote and secure equitable distribution of water amongst its members;
- maintain irrigation systems and ensure efficient, economical and equitable distribution and utilization of water to optimize agricultural production and
- protect the environment and ensure ecological balance.

The *Act* said that WUAs should actively involve the members, inculcating amongst them a sense of ownership of the irrigation system (Government of Maharashtra, 2005). Water will be provided only through the WUA to its members. They would benefit from assured water supply and can decide cropping patterns accordingly. It is their responsibility to administer the irrigation system and to collect charges to be financially self-sufficient. The Maharashtra Management of Irrigation Systems by Farmers Act also encourages WUAs to invest in improved irrigation technologies like drip and sprinkler systems, to develop farm ponds and community projects for exploiting groundwater, and to be engaged in additional income-earning activities like dairy and fisheries (Bhadwal, 2008). This is a substantial mandate for a new organization, but the WUAs seem to be developing well. The growth of WUAs in Maharashtra has been dramatic: in 2005 there were almost 800 in operation and more than 3,000 in various stages of implementation.

In total they cover about 1.5 million hectares, which is about 15 per cent of the irrigated area (Bhadwal, 2008).

McKay and Keremane (2006) found that WUAs in Maharashtra have been successful in devising and enforcing the rules for water distribution, fee collection and conflict resolution for over a decade. Naik and Kalro (2000) found that 82 per cent of farmers in the Mula scheme of Maharashtra and 74 per cent of farmers in the Bhima scheme in the same state ranked WUAs as their first choice for supplying water. The main reasons were assured water supply, fewer disputes among farmers, better maintenance and lack of corruption. The original control-oriented approach, relying on notifications and licences, ignores the possibility of decentralized water management that is better suited to local hydrological and social contexts.

Revenue Access and Spending Capacity

The financial capacity of the decentralized body controls what it will be able to do. In designing an adaptive policy using decentralized decision-making, financial capacity will be an important determinant of effectiveness. Fiscal constraints tend to result in local bodies receiving insufficient resources to manage the responsibilities which have been devolved to them. This can be a recipe for failure—the design of the mandate and the budget must be consistent.

There are several possible sources of revenue. The simplest is a direct grant from the government. This has a major advantage from the government's viewpoint in that the government can control the activities of the decentralized body through the budgeting process. The disadvantage, of course, is that possible leverage of other resources is not available, and thus the draw on the government's budget is larger than it might otherwise be, for a given level of activity. Beyond dedicated grants, there are several ways in which the decentralized body can raise revenue from other sources. In rough order of complexity, the body may; seek specific grants from government or other sources, charge fees for its services or have the capacity to charge taxes of some sort.

Specific grants were used by the Manitoba CDs to fund a variety of programmes. In addition to their operating grants, the CDs were able to apply to some of the wide variety of rural and agricultural support programmes that exist both at the national level and the provincial level. They were also able to approach the rural municipalities in their territory to seek support for activities. The flexibility inherent in this entrepreneurial capacity is further discussed in the following as a design issue.

For a body that provides services, user fees may be a source of funds. Such a system has several advantages: by paying for the service, users develop a stake in the organization and will be more involved; the decentralized body is able to cover costs in a way that relates to the level of service provided; and the draw on the government budget is reduced. In addition, of course, the normal argument for the pricing of natural resources applies.

The Maharashtra Water Users Associations charge for the water they provide to farmers. They are thus able to recover their operating costs, which include the cost of part of the irrigation water distribution system (Bhadwal, 2008).

Finally, the decentralized body may be given taxation authority. Municipal governments, school boards and a few other bodies have this authority in many countries, which provides them with the capacity to establish (with the consent of their voters) the level of services they will provide and pay for it from the taxation revenue. This is the most flexible system, in terms of both setting the size of the budget and deciding what to spend it on. While it introduces additional complexity, it has the advantage of strengthening accountability: public bodies that must fund their operations from taxes levied on citizens tend to be much more responsive to those citizens' wishes than if they are funded largely by grants (Ribot, 2004).

Given that the goal of the decentralization policy instrument is to increase the capacity of the policy to adapt well to unforeseen circumstances, it does not make sense to define too tightly how the decentralized body can spend its resources. While the budgetary approval process would give the opportunity to do this, the result would be exactly the sort of centralized decision-making that the instrument is designed to avoid. In other words, successful decentralization should include devolution of fiscal responsibility and authority.

Staff and Resources

A corollary to the budget discussion is the question of staffing levels and the availability of other resources such as offices, vehicles, computers, training and so on. All of these will need to be paid for, either directly by the decentralized body or provided by the government or other stakeholders. Examples of the latter would be seconded staff or office space provided without charge.

As with the other implementation issues discussed in this section, the decisions about staffing need to be taken in the context of the mandate being given to the decentralized body. The staff issue is not just how many people, but also with what experience, education and capacity. There may be a need for specific technical expertise to help manage canal systems, or perhaps watershed modelling capacity, experience with community outreach processes, and a general management capacity. One advantage of a centralized organization is that it will be larger and thus able to have more specialized experts on staff. However, an alternative management mechanism that the central organization can use is the provision of central specialized services. In addition to its possible efficiencies, this approach would allow the central body to be informed of what the decentralized bodies are doing, and also to ensure that technical tasks are competently executed.

Entrepreneurial Capacity

Since the nature of the unanticipated circumstances cannot, by definition, be forecasted in advance, the capacity to be entrepreneurial with regard to governance aspects such as partnerships and financing is critical to successful adaptive policies. For example, the Manitoba CDs are able to join partnerships, like the First Nations partnerships entered into by the Alonsa CD, which were not anticipated when the programme was designed (Barg and Oborne, 2006). Another example from the CDs is that of well capping. In this case, CDs solved a problem with abandoned wells, which were dangerous and a pollution risk, by finding government grants to pay for capping the wells. The grants came from several programmes—both federal and provincial—and the capacity of the local boards to apply for such funding and their entrepreneurial approach to finding such sources, provided a solution to a problem not foreseen when the CDs were formed (ibid.).

WHEN AND WHERE TO USE DECENTRALIZATION

Decentralization is a strategy for adaptive policy implementation. As such, it has to be considered in the policy design stage, but it conditions most aspects of implementation. Decentralization of planning, management or service delivery in the public sector can also be a huge policy reform in itself and has been the subject of numerous strategic policy studies. For recent examples see Cheema and Rondinelli (2007). But in the context of other substantive policy domains, as we use the term here, decentralization of policy delivery is an option for improving adaptability.

The choice of decentralized policy delivery depends on the framing of policy issues and objectives, and has sweeping implications for all other aspects of policy design. Decentralization is a sensible adaptive policy strategy when the interventions to address a policy problem are best tailored to diverse local conditions and when local capacities and resources are reasonably suited to the response task. For example, in the case of WUAs in Maharashtra, the management of water supply and delivery can be improved by matching it to local agricultural patterns (and vice versa). Manitoba CDs, with responsibility for planning and managing drainage infrastructure, are able to decide more quickly and equitably both on strategic priorities and on the merits of specific projects because there are fewer transaction costs to the input of knowledgeable local stakeholders in the decisions. So, for example, some CDs were able to identify and act upon unanticipated strategic opportunities to address emerging local priorities, such as rehabilitating old wells or joint planning with First Nations communities, because decision-making authority had been decentralized. Analogous arguments apply to the Irrigation Districts in Alberta, where decentralization of irrigation management provided opportunities for the Irrigation District to respond to local concerns about flooding and emergency planning and to take pre-emptive local measures to manage a severe drought. In all of these cases, the decision of the responsible government agencies to implement resource management policies in a decentralized fashion proved crucial to the local implementing agency's ability to respond adaptively and continue to fulfil their policy mandate in unanticipated conditions.

Decentralization is not appropriate for policy implementation when uniformity of policy implementation is a critical aspect of design, as for example in taxation or economic policy, which must apply equitably over a broad jurisdiction. But it is possible to decentralize some aspects of policy implementation when equitable application implies the need for local variation. So, for example, the three-level crop insurance delivery mechanism described earlier provides for equitable federal funding within a national agricultural policy framework, while allowing for diverse provincial priorities and coverage in accordance with local crop and risk patterns, and localized response to specific hazard events.

Decentralization also relies on local capacity for self-governance. Technical skills and capacity can be provided by senior government agencies on an advisory basis, but in the absence of accountable local governance structures and mechanisms, decentralization of decision-making is not a viable strategy. As an example, the implementation of soil and water conservation and sedentary agricultural strategies in Meghalaya province in India was not decentralized, but driven by the decisions of central- and state-level authorities through extension support and training, rather than responding to local leadership and decision-making authority.

Table 7.1 Overview of Decentralization of Decision-making

Decentralization of decision-making: Decentralizing the authority and responsibility for decision-making to the lowest effective and accountable unit of governance, whether existing or newly created, can increase the capacity of a policy to perform successfully when confronted with unforeseen events.

Why?	What is it?	How to apply it?	When to use it?
Having decisions made close to the citizens most affected is a way to provide better feedback and ensure that decision-makers are well informed about problems and effects of proposed interventions, as well as the nature of different interests in those problems and interventions. Because local conditions and ecosystems vary widely, decentralization provides a way to implement policy more flexibly when this is a key factor to ensure effectiveness and adaptation to change.	The transfer of responsibility for decision-making, along with appropriate resources and capacity, to a lower level of government or to a new institutional device.	The potential for decentralization in any particular policy area will depend on the scale of intervention needed, the extent of local knowledge and capacity, and the structure of governance mechanisms for accountability and coordination. Decentralization should consider the following in the context of the policy goals: • *governance system* to be used, including responsibility both to local stakeholders and to senior levels of government; • *geographic scope;* • the *decision-making scope* to be given to the decentralized body; • *access to revenues and the spending capacity* of the decentralized body; • *staffing and resources* to be given to it; and • the freedom of action and *entrepreneurial capacity* to be given to the decentralized body.	• Decentralization is a sensible adaptive policy tool when the interventions to address a policy problem are best tailored to diverse local conditions, and when local capacities and resources are reasonably suited to the response task. • It is incorporated in the policy design stage and realized during implementation.

This tool's greatest challenge is that it is seldom implemented because of political opposition to transfers of authority. Piecemeal or half-hearted decentralization typically results in the transfer of responsibility without sufficient authority, resources or scope for decision-making (Rondinelli, 1981). This makes it difficult for local bodies to actually learn from unexpected change and adapt to it. Even when appropriate powers are devolved, decentralization can also face challenges of sequencing the required reforms. For example, if management obligations are transferred before financial and revenue-generation powers are in place, this is likely to lead to failure. Transfer of technical responsibility without concomitant political responsibility will result in frustration, as power remains centralized but the work is done locally (Ribot, 2004).

Finally, it is important to recognize that using decentralization as a policy implementation strategy requires long-term commitment. The process leads to changes in roles and often structures of government at different levels and requires re-allocation of power between different agencies. This is never a simple or straightforward process and often takes many years to accomplish (Kemper et al., 2007).

LINKS TO OTHER ADAPTIVE POLICY TOOLS

One of the arguments for decentralized policy implementation is that it reduces the transaction costs of deliberative processes, which at a local level may involve fewer different interest groups and greater shared knowledge. Multi-stakeholder deliberation (Chapter 4) can then be employed more quickly and simply as a decision-making tool (for characterizing problems and issues or for policy implementation). Decentralized implementation can also help foster self-organization and social networking (Chapter 6), by building capacity and social capital for decision-making locally and identifying and removing barriers to spontaneous self-organized responses. A key rationale for decentralization is to promote variation between responses in different localities, so the tools described in Chapter 7 should be seen as complementary.

8 Promoting Variation

Sreeja Nair and Dimple Roy

What is variation? Given the complexity of most policy settings, implementing a variety of policies to address the same issue increases the likelihood of achieving desired outcomes. Diversity of responses also forms a common risk-management approach, facilitating the ability to perform efficiently in the face of unanticipated conditions.

WHY IS VARIATION IMPORTANT FOR ADAPTIVE POLICY-MAKING?

Individuals, groups, communities and systems have several defining characteristics that make them similar or different from each other. Some of these characteristics might be obvious, others not. Additionally, some characteristics might be latent, only to be revealed under stress at a later point in time (Axelrod and Cohen, 2000). This heterogeneity is instrumental in shaping the emergence of different responses from individuals, groups, communities and/ or systems even when exposed to the same stress. Diversity is indeed a key to understanding the structure and function of complex adaptive systems and enhancing their resilience to stress (Innes et al., 2005). The ability to deploy a number of different responses enables a community to spread risk and create buffers in the face of shocks and stresses (Berkes et al., 2003). For example, communities directly dependent on the natural resource base for livelihoods and sustenance are put at high risk by any change in climate. In particular, the ability of these vulnerable communities to cope with unanticipated climatic conditions is often compromised. Adaptive policy-making in this context should enhance the capability of vulnerable groups to spread risk by adopting a basket of livelihood options to enable them to survive even if some options fail (Ellis, 2000).

If there are mechanisms to ensure that the end-users are safeguarded against any possible negative spin-offs, then exploration of new and innovative ideas and strategies can be made easier and less risky (Axelrod and Cohen, 2000). Focusing on one solution to a policy problem also runs the risk of incurring losses under conditions of specific stresses. For example, monocultures may be completely wiped out due to attack by particular pests, compared to a mixed cropping pattern where some crops might survive. Furthermore, any strategy that has a myopic focus and reduces the scope for variation faces a high risk of failure, especially when the strategy is based on an unreliable, uncertain hypothesis (Moench and Dixit, 2007).

WHAT IS PROMOTING VARIATION?

Variation in the policy realm simply means that several options are being used to achieve an intended outcome. Variation can be viewed as several 'parallel experiments' being undertaken simultaneously with the aim of achieving a common objective. Glouberman et al. (2003) recommend that policy interventions should *promote variation* because '*introducing small-scale interventions for the same problem offers greater hope of finding effective solutions*'. This is based on the understanding that 'many interventions will fail and that such *failures are simply a feature of how one develops successful interventions* in complex adaptive systems' (ibid.). Within the context of adaptive policy-making, variation can promote learning, foster innovation, enhance performance and accelerate the rate of delivery of critical services (that may include sanitation, drinking water, health, education, and so on) (Ellerman, 2004).

The different options facilitated through adaptive policies might be interpreted and adopted by the communities in different ways and might achieve varying degrees of success, depending on how the communities perceive, use and develop each policy option. Promoting variation in order to stimulate responses to the same problem might be a combination of several different strategies. For example, in response to a stressor such as drought, communities might adopt some common or traditional strategies such as planting drought-hardy crops, temporarily migrating to nearby areas or adopting alternate income-generation activities (that are less climate-sensitive).

Based on region-specific dynamics vulnerable communities might be able to take advantage of available opportunities and resources to foster innovative response mechanisms to stress. Such opportunities might include striking linkages with private players and benefiting from a crop buy-back facility or from monitoring systems providing reliable climatic and agriculture-related information. In Maharashtra, India, for example, Participatory Watershed Management has attempted to address the equity issue while promoting variation (Tomar and Nair, 2008). In order to address the landless and marginal farmers, specific financial provisions have been provided for livestock, particularly for fodder cultivation, preventive medication, primary healthcare of cattle and capacity building. Major project investment was made on large engineering structures like check dams in the lower reaches of drainage lines, which only benefited rich farmers in the villages. By promotion of livestock and emphasis on training and capacity building of the village communities, the policy has attempted to target other farmers as well. Under the revised guidelines, funds were earmarked for activities like awareness and capacity building and training of communities in order to ensure balanced utilization of funds.

An overview of variation as an adaptive policy-making tool is provided in Table 8.1.

HOW TO PROMOTE VARIATION

Promoting variation requires that the policy-maker assumes different roles. First, the policy-maker can perform the role of an architect, designing and implementing a variety of policy options. Second, the policy-maker can be a facilitator, creating an enabling environment for variation to occur. And third, the policy-maker can be a learner, studying from past and current experiences and adapting as needed. With any of these three roles, there is a need for the policy-maker to consider certain underlying principles. These include:

- *Articulation of the end goal(s)*: By articulating the policy goal, designing a variety of options for addressing a particular problem becomes easier.
- *Understanding scale*: It is essential to understand the scale of operation in order to promote variation. The concept of scale is useful to measure differences across space, time, jurisdictions or institutions (Cash et al., 2006). Understanding scale is essential in order to identify indicators to determine suitable response options for deployment, and to understand the homogeneity and heterogeneity between target communities.

Policy-maker as the Architect

The policy-maker acting as an *architect* can promote variation by designing and implementing a range of alternative options to meet the diverse needs of different stakeholders. This can be facilitated by: (1) using a mix of policy instruments; (2) exploring synergies with other policies; (3) providing opportunities for risk-spreading and (4) undertaking cost-benefit analysis.

Using a mix of policy instruments

The policy-maker can promote variation directly by designing and implementing a mix of policy instruments that have good potential for helping achieve the intended outcome. Instruments available to policy-makers include: economic (for example, taxes, subsidies and tradable permits); regulatory (for example, laws); expenditures (for example, research and development, education and awareness); and institutional (for example, sustainable development strategies).

We observed a good example of using a mix of policy instruments in the Government of Canada's new Agricultural Policy Framework, 'Growing Forward' in 2008 (Swanson et al., 2008). Growing Forward programmes were developed based on consultations with over 3,000 participants from across the country. The programmes are guided by a vision for a profitable and innovative agriculture, agrifood and agriculture-based products industry that seizes opportunities in responding to growing market demands and contributes to the health and well-being of Canadians (AAFC, 2008). The new suite of programmes is designed to be more responsive, predictable and bankable for farmers. The new approach advances agricultural stabilization policy into the proactive realm of risk management. The four programmes that form the business risk-management approach are: AgriInvest, providing coverage for small income declines and allows for investments that help mitigate risks or improve market income; AgriStability, providing support when a producer experiences larger farm income losses; AgriRecovery, providing a coordinated process for federal, provincial and territorial governments to respond rapidly when disasters strike, filling gaps not covered by existing programmes; and AgriInsurance, an existing programme that includes insurance against production losses for specified perils (weather, pests, disease) and is being expanded to include more commodities (AAFC, 2007).

Taken together, these programmes represent the federal government's proposal to replace the safety net approach with a more adaptive risk-management approach. Such a risk management set of policies can collectively offer a resilient safety net; in part because of the diversity of instruments. Hence there is a need to encourage the evolution of such policy sets by an understanding of community needs and capacities.

Exploring synergies with other policies

As an architect, a policy-maker can also promote variation by identifying linkages with other policies and instruments that: might already exist to address the issue; or are being implemented to address a different outcome, but yet have an indirect positive impact on the issue at hand. There are often policies that have co-benefits for the objectives of other policies. For example, policies related to public healthcare also have spillover effects on the objectives of disaster management policies. By fostering synergies with other policies, a variety of options can be made available to stakeholders. For this it is essential that every policy has a component under which they review the points of commonalities with other sectoral or regional policies or programmes.

Providing opportunities for risk-spreading

Focusing on one solution to a policy problem might cause losses under conditions of specific stresses. For example, monocultures may be completely wiped out due to attack by particular pests, compared to a mixed cropping pattern, where some crops might survive. Ellis (1999), in studying sustainable livelihoods, concludes that diversification helps to overcome the uncertainty of seasonality (for example, droughts) and can contribute towards creation of alternative sources of income-generation during non-season periods. For example, a farmer who can diversify the sources from which he derives his income can do better when faced with climatic shocks and stresses than a farmer who depends completely on agriculture for income. For example, the Watershed Development Program in Shifting Cultivation areas in Meghalaya (India) identifies several integrated development components, for example, natural resources management, rehabilitation component, service sector and livestock system. This programme also has financial provisions for transport of agricultural produce to the markets, convergence of various activities and schemes, and financial provisions for livestock and fodder cultivation, thereby encouraging the diversification of livelihoods existing in the community.

Performing cost-benefit analyses

There needs to be a careful exploration of the costs and benefits of diversity in order to adjudge the right portfolio strategy to minimize risk while maximizing benefits. Furthermore, there is a need to consider costs versus benefits of implementing a variety of options and alternatives. Cost-benefit analyses can help in avoiding costs associated with investing in policies that fail and/or use of policies that are less than optimal under emerging circumstances.

The Policy-maker as Facilitator: Creating an Enabling Environment for Variation

Acting as a *facilitator* the policy-maker does not actually control what happens, but creates an enabling environment for variation to occur. Hence, the role of the policy-maker in this context is to facilitate conditions that enable societies to create alternative approaches to achieve a common objective, or in response to a common issue, and requires being a 'facilitator of learning' rather than being a 'trainer' (Ellerman, 2004). These actions include: (1) identifying influencing factors and (2) removing barriers and facilitating variation.

Leverage key influencing factors

To enable communities to adopt different solutions in response to the same issue, it is essential to identify factors that can promote variation and those that can hinder it. Chapter 6 on enabling self-organization and social networks describes how such conditions can be facilitated. For example:

- The facilitating factors can include presence and development of information infrastructure and ensuring access to resources that can enable development of innovative responses.
- It is essential to understand the role of social capital and networks for the success of any policy tool.
- Information sharing and dissemination can be extremely useful in encouraging the community to adopt a particular alternative.

Removing barriers and facilitating variation

Barriers that can hinder adoption of selected options by the target communities need to be identified and removed. These barriers may include lack of awareness, education, inequity, lack of resources, and appropriate institutional structures and governance mechanisms. Incentives need to be provided to encourage adoption of identified options. Furthermore, incentives can also foster innovation and enable communities to develop solutions based on their capacities. These incentives could be in the form of subsidies and innovation funds to promote targeted activities in response to stresses. In India, for example, weather-indexed crop insurance is being implemented on a pilot basis for various crops and locations through different types of delivery modes. This scheme seeks to protect the farmers' overall income, rather than being restricted to yield from a specific crop. The pilots launched on an experimental basis offer benefits in the form of an opportunity to better understand the risk patterns, exploring the potential of the pilot for commercial expansion, creating awareness and building trust among the beneficiaries, i.e., the farmers, and incorporating customer feedback to make the pilot model user-friendly and efficient for risk minimization.

The Policy-maker as a Learner

As a *learner*, perceiving and incorporating valuable feedback from the ground level of policy implementation is the core function of the policy-maker.

Learning by doing

There is a need to identify best practices or innovative options that have worked well and to strengthen these policies. These successes should be communicated and publicized to facilitate copying by other jurisdictions. Furthermore, successful stories can be custom-tailored and adapted on a region-specific and target-group-specific basis. Chapter 9 addresses the practice of formal policy review and continuous learning for adaptive policies. For example, in the implementation of Participatory Watershed Management in Maharashtra, India, the Ministry of Agriculture and Ministry of Rural Development jointly prepared common guidelines for the implementation of their respective watershed development projects (Tomar and Nair, 2008). These common guidelines provide for the engagement of a wide range of organizations such as non-governmental organizations (NGOs), agriculture research institutions and various government departments and Panchayati Raj Institutions. These guidelines consolidate the lessons learned and experiences gained to facilitate the planning, implementation and monitoring of the programme and hence attempt to bring various activities to a common goal. Based on what has worked best on ground, the guidelines mention that scientific expertise from research institutions, technical and managerial know-how of the project staff, and accumulated experience of the village community should be symbiotically integrated to finalize the choice of treatments in the watersheds.

WHEN AND WHERE TO APPLY VARIATION

During the policy design cycle, the policy-maker operates as an architect by first identifying and characterizing the probable conditions of risk (for example, in terms of impacts on vulnerable systems or communities and extent of impact). Scenario analysis and planning methods can be used for identifying such risks (see Chapter 3). The next step would be to identify a set of alternative response strategies that can be undertaken to minimize the impacts from the identified or projected risks. It is essential to note that the role of policy-makers would be to understand the resources or skill-sets required for the deployment of each of these alternative strategies and to facilitate adoption and deployment of these strategies through appropriate policies to minimize risks. With greater certainty or advancement in technology and development, this set of alternatives can be upgraded to achieve a greater level of efficiency and ease of applicability via regular monitoring, evaluation and improvement.

During policy implementation, the role of the policy-maker is that of a facilitator, that is, the policy-maker should facilitate the smooth transition of each of identified response strategies into the operation phase and remove the barriers that hinder the adoption of these strategies. Furthermore, a comparative analysis of the costs of implementation and benefits accrued on implementation of each of the strategies needs to be undertaken in a regular manner to update on the efficiency of each of the strategies as newer conditions unfold and emerge.

Common to both the design and implementation is the role of the policy-maker as a learner. At different stages of the policy cycle, it is critical for the policy-maker to monitor and evaluate the policy instruments deployed to promote variation, as well as to incorporate feedback from the grassroots level where variation needs to be promoted.

Other considerations. There are certain considerations that the policy-maker needs to understand while assuming the role of an architect, facilitator and/or a learner. Overlapping domains of functionality within the government departments and ministries might often hinder identification of the end goal towards which a variety of response strategies need to be developed.

In terms of identifying synergies between different government domains, policy-makers might face uncertainty with respect to identifying evolution of future structures within the government or changes in roles and responsibilities within the hierarchical institutional framework.

Time considerations might make it difficult to identify effective strategies in terms of time required to observe success/failure and obtain feedback from the communities in order to decide whether to continue implementation of that strategy.

Variation can also face risks depending on the level of knowledge of decision-makers, access to information and perception. It is also essential to note that, the perceptions of risk vary and consequently the appropriate policy responses vary (Doss et al., 2006). For example, among the factors influencing a farmer's decision to bring variation at the farm level include perception of risk, management and production skills, availability of labour, ownership of fixed assets, seasonality issues, consumer preferences and expected returns. If the risks are perceived to be high, it can imply that it is less likely that communities try different options. It is useful because communities can choose by judging how suitable a particular option is, while at the same time, it might be difficult for the government to make people invest in a particular option. To reduce this discrepancy, the government needs to provide complete information to the communities. It is essential to strike a balance between development of current strategies and exploring newer options (Axelrod and Cohen, 2000). This is important because exploration of new options over and above the existing strategies have costs associated with them. Given that these options may or may not be successful, it is essential to understand limits to diversification while promoting variation.

If there are mechanisms to ensure that the end-users are safeguarded against possible negative impacts, then exploration of new and innovative ideas and strategies can be made easier and less risky (ibid.).

LINKS TO OTHER ADAPTIVE POLICY TOOLS

To design/facilitate variation it is essential for the policy-maker to know the existing socio-economic conditions and the conditions of environmental (or climatic) stress that are likely in the future. For this purpose, it is essential to receive inputs on a range of integrated plausible future scenarios—this forms the link with the tools of integrated and forward-looking analysis (Chapter 3) and multi-stakeholder deliberation (Chapter 4).

We saw in Chapter 6 that enabling self-organization and social networking brings together 'agents of change' to foster emergence of innovative responses to unanticipated events. This also helps promote variation by creating opportunities for sharing of experiences between diverse groups. This process of learning from each other can result in the evolution of a variety of ideas, finding genesis from the risk management domain, but being diverse in terms of modes and modalities of their execution, hence providing a set of diverse solutions for the same problem.

Table 8.1 Overview of Promoting Variation

What is promoting variation? Given the complexity of most policy settings, implementing a variety of policies to address the same issue increases the likelihood of achieving desired outcomes. Diversity of responses also forms a common risk-management approach, facilitating the ability to perform efficiently in the face of unanticipated conditions.

Why?	What is it?	How to apply it?	When to use it?
• Diversity forms the key to understanding the structure and function of complex adaptive systems and enhancing their resilience to stress (Innes et al., 2005). • Promoting variation and enhancing diversity enables a community to spread risk and create buffers in the face of shocks and stresses (Berkes et al., 2003).	The policy-maker as an *architect*: • Providing a range of policy options • Designing and using a mix of policy instruments to achieve a single policy objective • Seeing and making linkages with other policies that have similar intent The policy-maker as a *facilitator*: • Creating an enabling environment for variation to occur The policy-maker as a *learner*: • Observing which policies work well and strengthening those policies	• Making use of a balance of economic instruments (for example, taxes, tradable permits); regulatory instruments (for example, laws); expenditure instruments (for example, R&D, education and awareness); and institutional instruments (for example, cross-sectoral plans) • Exploring synergies with other policies • Providing opportunities for risk-spreading • Undertaking cost-benefit analysis • Identifying influencing factors such as access to information; enabling self-organization and social networking (see Chapter 6); and information sharing • Removing barriers and facilitating variation • Learn by doing, using processes for formal policy review and continuous learning (see Chapter 9)	Policy design and implementation Policy set-up Policy set-up, design and implementation Policy monitoring, review and improvement stage

Similarly, in Chapter 7, we were reminded that placing decision-making authority at the lowest effective jurisdictional level, where the impacts are felt most, helps a policy to adapt to unanticipated issues. Governance structures and decentralization mechanisms might differ from place to place thereby affecting variation. Furthermore, since these alternative response strategies operate as 'parallel experiments', there needs to be continuous monitoring, evaluation and improvement of each of these strategies in order to improve their efficiency in terms of risk minimization under unanticipated conditions. This is enabled through the mechanism of formal policy review and continuous learning as described next in Chapter 9. Formal policy review also helps in determining which interventions are actually working and which are not.

9 Formal Policy Review and Continuous Learning

Sanjay Tomar and Darren Swanson

What are formal policy review and continuous learning? Regular review, even when the policy is performing well, and the use of well-designed pilots throughout the life of the policy to test assumptions related to performance, can help address emerging issues and trigger important policy adjustments.

WHY ARE FORMAL POLICY REVIEW AND CONTINUOUS LEARNING IMPORTANT FOR ADAPTIVE POLICY?

In Chapter 3 we introduced the case example of the Crow Rate, a rate-control agreement for transporting grain produced on the Canadian Prairies by railway. This policy instrument was a fixture of western Canadian agriculture and development for almost 100 years. It was engraved into the Railway Act in 1925 and did not change for the next 60 years. The history of the policy was relatively quiet up to the end of World War II, but inflation eventually began to erode the railway's revenues. The performance of the system suffered significantly, which became painfully apparent when Canada's grain export market expanded to Russia and China. Public pressure began to mount in response to the deterioration of the rail system, sparking at least seven commissions, studies and inquiries from 1960 through 1982 to better understand the extent of the issue and the range of impacts. Following the seventh study in 1982, the stress had built up enough to result in a complete policy overhaul with the introduction of the Western Grain Transportation Act.

It is safe to say in a retrospective analysis of the Canadian Crow Rate, that if an annual formal review process had been required as part of the policy, it would have been possible to detect more quickly the deterioration of the rail transportation system. The *ad hoc* nature of the protracted series of commissions and studies that did occur, were not effective in bringing about incremental changes in the Crow Rate over time. The impacts cumulated and the policy eventually reached a breaking point and had to be completely overhauled.

In his account of managing the development of hydro-electric power and restoration of the salmon fishery in the Columbia River Basin in the Pacific northwest of the United States, Kai Lee described his notion of formal review and continuous learning. He concludes that adaptive policies should test clearly formulated hypotheses about the behaviour of an ecosystem being changed by human use (Lee, 1993). His notion involves understanding at the outset that the policy will need to learn and likely be refined based on the observed outcomes.

In this regard, Holling (1978) outlined eight broad lessons that emerged from his analysis of complex socio-economic and ecologic systems, mostly informed by the organized connection between parts of a system, their spatial heterogeneity, resilience and dynamic variability. These lessons provide important rationales for why formal review and continuous learning is necessary for policy interventions. These lessons are:

- Since everything is not intimately connected to everything else, there is no need to measure everything. There is a need, however, to determine the significant connections.
- Structural features (size, distribution, age, who connects to whom) are more important to measure than numbers.
- Changes in one variable can have unexpected impacts on variables at the same place but several connections away.
- Events at one place can re-emerge as impacts at distant places.
- Monitoring the wrong variable can seem to indicate no change even when drastic change is imminent.
- Impacts are not necessarily immediate and gradual; they can appear abruptly some time after the event.
- Variability of ecological systems, including occasional major disruptions, provides a kind of self-monitoring system that maintains resilience. Polices that reduce variability in space or time, even in an effort to improve environmental quality, should always be questioned.
- Many existing impact assessment methods (for example, cost-benefit analysis, input output, cross-impact matrices, linear models and discounting) assume none of the above occurs or, at least, that none is important.

Such observations are not just unique to natural resources management. The healthcare sector also deals with such complexity in policy interventions. Glouberman et al. (2003) learned that in working within complex adaptive systems, possible solutions undergo selection by the system itself. They therefore stress the importance of 'evaluating performance of potential solutions', and based on this evaluation, 'selecting the best candidates for further support and development'.

WHAT ARE FORMAL POLICY REVIEW AND CONTINUOUS LEARNING?

Formal review is a similar category of adaptive policy tool to automatic adjustment, in that it acknowledges that monitoring and remedial measures are integral to complex adaptive systems (Holling, 1978) and that it is necessary to constantly refine interventions through a continual process of variation and selection (Glouberman et al., 2003). Yet formal review is fundamentally different from automatic adjustment. Automatic adjustment can anticipate what signposts to use and what actions might need to be triggered to keep the policy effective. Formal review, on the other hand, is a mechanism for identifying and dealing with unanticipated circumstances and emerging issues.

There is also a subtle, yet fundamental, difference between formal review and *ad hoc* review. While *ad hoc* review will always remain an important aspect of policy learning and continuous adaptation, it is the intent of this mechanism to emphasize the greater role that systematic or regularly scheduled formal review plays in policy learning and adaptation. Both can accomplish the intended result—that being critical policy adaptations—but *ad hoc* review relies often on a long process of public opinion and debate before a formal review and a needed policy adjustment are triggered. Formal reviews in the context of this category are preset processes that occur even if the policy appears to be performing well. This regularly scheduled assessment process can be very useful in detecting emerging issues that can impact on the policy's performance.

In this guidebook, we articulate a process of policy review and continuous learning that must be formally built into the policy cycle (Table 9.1). We describe the formal review and continuous learning mechanisms according to three aspects: (1) the types of *triggers* for the review; (2) the types of *review* that can result in policy learning and (3) the types of *improvements* that can be made based on the learning.

The Triggers

There are several ways in which formal review, as described in this book, can be triggered. The first is based on a *pre-defined time interval* such as annual or bi-annual. This type of trigger is meant to help detect and track emerging issues, because with such a time trigger, a review will occur even when the policy is working well and there may be no apparent need for a review to be undertaken.

For example, when Canada's Crow Rate policy needed a major overhaul following 60 years of inflexible policy and *ad hoc* reviews, the new Western Grain Transportation Act mandated that regular reviews be conducted every four years by the National Transportation Agency to take account of productivity and costing changes. Time-triggered review is also a part of India's Five-Year National Plan process. This plan is formally reviewed once during the midpoint of plan implementation to monitor progress and to modify the plan if necessary.

But a time-triggered review may not be of sufficient periodicity under certain circumstances. If an unanticipated event occurs midway through a year and policy adjustment becomes necessary to avoid unintended impacts and ensure that policy outcomes remain on target, a second type of trigger is needed. Indicators of system performance, often called signposts (Ralston and Wilson, 2006; Walker and Marchau, 2003), are helpful in this regard. Triggers are discussed in Chapter 5 on *automatic* policy adjustment mechanisms. In Chapter 5 we described a spectrum of policy review that starts with a *fully-automatic* adjustment in which the policy adjustment could be pre-defined. But pre-defining the adjustment is not always possible, and some additional analysis is necessary to formulate the adjustment. Extending the spectrum further, in some instances the analysis to define a policy adjustment might expose deeper issues that will require a more comprehensive and deliberative review of the policy. The latter type of review is the subject of this chapter. The triggering indicators are essentially the same as discussed in Chapter 5; however, the formal review is initiated at a request resulting from an expert analysis that was attempting to formulate a policy adjustment.

Given the complexity of most policy issues it is typically not possible to develop and track enough system performance indicators to detect the array of unanticipated circumstances. For this reason, the systematic tracking and distillation of *stakeholder feedback* is critically important for formal review and continuous improvement. The capacity to compile and study this feedback should not be under-emphasized. While complaints are one form of stakeholder feedback, another is the availability of new information that typically comes from social and natural scientists. Reviewing and distilling this information is time intensive, but the signals this type of information can provide can be prescient and critical for seeing the unanticipated issues that lie just around the corner.

The Review Process

Formal policy review is meant to assess if the assumptions for how the policy was intended to perform were accurate, and to study and implement any necessary changes to the policy. Ideally it should be both an analytical and a deliberative process to understand cause-and-effect relationships and to detect unintended impacts of the policy. The review process can also be in the form of a policy pilot to test out a policy on a smaller scale to assess its potential impact and how implementation mechanisms will perform.

For example, over the past three decades, India has addressed soil and water conservation through a mix of technological innovations, participatory approaches and an enabling policy environment. The participatory watershed management policy is reviewed on an interim-period basis by the Government of India and the necessary modifications are incorporated during India's national Five-Year Plan process. Apart from the review by the Planning Commission, the Ministry of Agriculture and Cooperation, and the Ministry of Rural Development have also reviewed the performance of specific watershed developments projects (Hanumantha Rao, 2000; Joshi et al., 2000, 2004; Joy et al., 2005; Kerr et al., 2004) in India and have diagnosed various limitations based on the lessons learned from project implementation and pilot projects.

The Canada Pension Plan (CPP) provides a good example of an *analytical review* that is conducted triennially. The 2006 review confirmed that the CPP is on sound financial footing—Canada's Minister of Finance reported that 'Our analysis suggests that the 9.9 per cent contribution rate will be sufficient to sustain the Plan into the foreseeable future.... We have therefore agreed that the contribution rate will remain unchanged' (Ministry of Finance, Canada, 2006).[1] The review did suggest however, that some changes to how the Plan operates will be necessary and that the policy should be reviewed again to ensure that the proposed changes are integrated and the policy is working well.

The review process can also be more consultative including a group of stakeholders and experts. For example, the Planning Commission, Government

---

[1] See http://www.fin.gc.ca/news06/06-026e.html

of India, formed a Working Group on 'Watershed Development, Rainfed Farming and Natural Resources Management' for the formulation of the Tenth Five-Year Plan (2002–07). This included a review of various ongoing schemes and projects in the sphere of natural resources management, particularly the programmes based on a watershed development approach under the Ministries of Agriculture, Rural Development, and Environment and Forests. The existing projects and programmes were examined to identify their strengths, weaknesses, constraints and bottlenecks and to suggest appropriate measures for the Tenth Five-Year Plan to achieve sustainable development.

A type of formal review was observed in our case study of the Saskatchewan Soil Conservation Association (SSCA) in Canada (Roy et al., 2007). At its annual conference, the SSCA takes stock of its functions and determines its future path and actions. This allows various stakeholders to deliberate certain issues even when there is no perceived need for it. As an example, the SSCA has gradually shifted its extension focus from zero-tillage for soil conservation to also include carbon sequestration and climate change mitigation as part of the shifting priorities of the federal and provincial governments. While some of this movement has been related to priority shifts in funding sources, the SSCA board of directors and staff has also realized the value of 'keeping up with the times' and enabling zero-tillage uptake with all its benefits (ibid.).

Ideally the formal review should occur within the context of a scenario analysis and planning process. As outlined previously in Chapter 3, such a process creates testing situations to study how a policy would perform under plausible future conditions. When a scenario planning process has been used to design a policy, it can provide the context for the regular formal policy review process, to assess which plausible futures are unfolding and which types of policy adjustments might be needed in the near future. For example, in creating the South Saskatchewan Basin Water Allocation Regulation (1991), the Alberta government demonstrated the use of a forward-looking review mechanism (Swanson et al., 2008). The regulation set the maximum amount of water that can be allocated for irrigation in each Irrigation District. However, the maximum allocations were recognized as approximations based on partial scientific knowledge. The government, therefore, committed to reviewing the regulation in 2000 because of the 'limitations of the databases and estimates of current and future water uses' (IWMSC, 2002: 21). As a result, Alberta Environment issued an 'Approved Water Management Plan for the South Saskatchewan River Basin' in August 2006.

One particular form of review process that is different than described in the foregoing is the *policy pilot*. A recent review conducted by the UK Cabinet Office (2003) focused on the role of pilot studies in policy-making. The study noted that 'an important innovation in recent years has been the phased introduction of major government policies or programmes, allowing them to be tested, evaluated, and adjusted where necessary, before being rolled out nationally' (ibid.: 3). The study noted that the practice of policy pilots has been relatively wide spread in the United States owing in part to its federal structure, which in many instances has implemented and evaluated a policy within one state before being rolled out nationally.

The study recommends the following:

The full-scale introduction of new policies and delivery mechanisms should, wherever possible, be preceded by closely monitored pilots. Phased introduction not only helps to inform implementation, but also to identify and prevent unintended consequences. A pilot is an important first stage of regular, longer-term policy monitoring and evaluation.

(ibid.)

The purpose of a policy pilot should be clearly outlined at the outset to ensure that the appropriate methods and timing can be established (ibid.). The purpose could be to test the likely impact of the policy or to test processes related to implementation.

The practice of policy piloting was and still is common in the crop insurance industry. The early days of crop insurance in the United States adopted a trial approach after several policy failures. The experience in the United States likely influenced the Manitoba Crop Insurance Review Committee in Canada to recommend in 1954 that a crop insurance programme make use of *test areas*. Their report cited that 'certain groups favoured the setting up of test areas in which a crop insurance program could be trialed out and, if necessary modified before it was adopted throughout the province' (MCIC, 1954: 14). Evidence of institutionalizing this type of policy testing was seen in the changes to the Manitoba Crop Insurance Program introduced for 2007. Two policy pilot programmes were initiated: Pasture Drought Insurance Pilot Program and the Fall Frost Insurance Pilot Program (MASC, 2007a, 2007b). In these programmes, data from weather stations trigger indemnity payments (see Chapter 5). The mechanism for testing these automatic policy adjustment features was a pilot programme, designed to 'to evaluate the need for a weather derivative type insurance program'. In India, weather-indexed insurance (see Chapter 5) was implemented on a pilot basis for various crops and locations by trying out different types of delivery models. The implementing agencies in India, ICICI Lombard and BASIX, have reported that this pilot experience was valuable to better understand risk parameters and the potential for commercial expansion (Kelkar, 2006). It was also an opportunity to create awareness among farmers, build trust through timely payouts and improve the design in response to customer feedback. Moreover, the early pilot schemes offered by the private sector were followed by the entry of the public sector.

Perhaps the most important aspect of the policy pilot is that it 'should be undertaken in the spirit of experimentation. If it is clear at the outset that a new policy and its delivery mechanisms are effectively already cast in stone, a pilot is redundant and ought not to be undertaken' (UK Cabinet Office, 2003).

While we discuss policy pilots in the foregoing discussion as a discrete activity to be conducted before scaling up a particular policy, we are essentially advocating in this chapter that an adaptive policy is one that is always open to revision when new information as to impacts, effectiveness and future implications becomes available. That is, the policy is 'tested, evaluated, and adjusted where necessary' (ibid.) on a continuous basis, triggered either by a specified time interval, the monitoring of key system indicators or by stakeholder feedback.

Policy Improvement

The point of a formal review is to make necessary policy adjustments. This includes identifying new signpost indicators and associated threshold values that can trigger future policy adjustments or terminate the policy if it is no longer relevant. This point is made quite explicitly in the context of policy pilots. The UK study stressed that 'appropriate mechanisms should always be in place to adapt (or abandon) a policy or its delivery mechanism in light of a pilot's findings'.

This speaks directly to the notion of adaptive policy-making presented by Walker et al. (2001) and summarized in Chapter 2: that learning and adaptation of the policy must be made 'explicit at the outset' and the inevitable 'policy changes to become part of a larger, recognized process and not forced to be made repeatedly on an *ad hoc* basis'.

Therefore, the type of formal policy review process that we advocate in this chapter is one that establishes an intimate link between the review and the recommended improvement. That is, that policy review and adjustment are an integral and expected part of policy implementation.

For example, in Maharashtra, India, the Vaidyanathan Committee on Pricing of Irrigation Water, 1992, critically assessed the coverage and impact of Water Users Associations (WUAs). The Ninth Five-Year Plan (1999–2002) and the Maharashtra Water and Irrigation Commission (1999) formulated strategies to increase farmer participation in irrigation management. The mid-term appraisal of the Tenth Five-Year Plan (2002–07) reviewed the progress of takeover of irrigation systems by WUAs. It found that there were about 55,000 WUAs covering 10 million hectares, and aimed to increase this 8–10 times in order to cover all irrigated area. Except for Gujarat, it found that in most states revenue departments continued to collect charges and pass on a portion to WUAs for system maintenance. It has called for empowerment of WUAs to set tariffs and retain a part of them, understanding barriers and simultaneously rehabilitating them so that they are in a position to invest in infrastructure repairs and improvement.

HOW TO USE FORMAL POLICY REVIEW AND CONTINUOUS LEARNING IN ADAPTIVE POLICY-MAKING

Triggering a Review

We discussed previously that a formal review can be triggered in three ways: (1) by a specified time period; (2) through the monitoring of system perform-ance indicators and (3) by stakeholder feedback, including new scientific information.

The required periodicity of a *time-triggered review* depends primarily on the level of risk associated with policy failure and on the pace of change in policy parameters and intended outcomes. For example, in the Canada Pension Plan case, while the risk of policy failure is quite high (retired persons not getting their promised retirement benefit), the pace at which key policy parameters are anticipated to change is relatively slow. So in this case a triennial review periodicity may suffice. In other situations, a longer period between reviews is considered appropriate. As a general rule of thumb, though, somewhere between an annual and a five year review is recommended for most policies.

In situations where the performance of a policy is highly sensitive to a certain input parameter, or where the impacts of the policy are potentially serious, but uncertain, the use of system performance indicators as *signposts to trigger the review*, in addition to time-triggers, is merited. These signpost indicators can be identified using scenario analysis (Chapter 3).

Stakeholder feedback always has and always will be an important part of policy review. It can be encouraged through specific efforts to strengthen the value of feedback by explicitly requesting and responding to it. Even without such solicitation, however, there will always be some sort of stakeholder feedback. In this case, it will be an *ad hoc* process, but we do believe that strengthening and adding a degree of formality to this process can strengthen this triggering mechanism. In most cases, stakeholder feedback is directed at the political offices (that is, the minister's office) in the form of letters, phone calls, emails and statements in the media (for example, newspaper, television, radio). The feedback is then channelled to the appropriate technical persons within the bureaucracy. These processes for reviewing stakeholder feedback, however, are typically under-resourced.

We advocate that each policy should have an identified expert team that reviews feedback received on the policy and that has the necessary capacity to analyze responses and devise good ways to respond to them. Reviewed on an individual basis, stakeholder feedback is often seen as a host of complaints that cannot all be addressed. But taken in aggregate, a set of seemingly unrelated complaints may actually be telling an important story about an emerging issue or an unintended consequence of a policy instrument. An assigned policy review team for stakeholder feedback would ideally be trained in methods of integrated and forward-looking analysis (Chapter 3) and would be able to use systems thinking to detect key messages.

Conducting the Review

The review process itself is best undertaken using both analytic and deliberative processes (see Chapters 3 and 4, respectively). And, perhaps most importantly, it requires open and transparent access to information. These requirements differ considerably from current practices where an expert culture with private access to information typically prevails. Formal review needs to be transparent so that the learning can be incorporated. Necessary for this transparency are the following: new information must be available, consciously collected (for example, indicators of performance or change) and monitored over appropriate time scales; and change must be possible and must be implemented in ways that are open and understandable to all actors (Pahl-Wostl, 2008).

Given that different agencies are often responsible for policy design and implementation, it is important that the formal review and continuous improvement approach advocated in this chapter include both policy designers and implementers. This is to provide perspectives on process and on policy impact.

Since the process needs to address *unanticipated* circumstances, its mandate and analysis should be wide-ranging and encourage creativity. Questions to be considered should include:

- *Goals:* Are the previously set goals still relevant? If not, what changes may be appropriate?
- *Current impacts of policy:* Is the policy as currently implemented having the intended impacts? Is the policy having unintended social, environmental or economic impacts? Consideration should be given both to policy design and to its practical delivery.
- *Emerging factors affecting policy:* Are there new factors foreseen that might affect the efficiency or effectiveness of the policy in meeting its goals or cause the policy to have unintended impacts? What are the anticipated impacts of existing policy, given these emerging factors?
- *Overlap:* Does the existing policy overlap with other policies, including those from other levels of government or jurisdictions?
- *Management and administrative issues:* How could management and administration be improved?
- *Pilots:* What additional policy pilots or research tests are needed to better inform new policy instrument design and implementation?
- *New policy design:* Do new policy instruments recommended by the review process address issues of overlap, efficiency, and so on?

Effective communication is essential if the analysis is to have an impact on decision-making. Holling (1978) explains that at least as much effort must go into communication as goes into the analysis itself. Individuals involved in doing an environmental assessment are generally not involved in the decision-making. They instead comprise an advisory body that formulates and presents conclusions to the decision-making body. An analyst who wishes to convey the results of a detailed study faces a serious dilemma. The volume of information is usually very large, in the hopes that the decision-maker will have the time to absorb and assess it. In order to achieve successful communication, the assessors must clarify what information there is and to whom it should be transferred. The format or technique of communication depends on the answers to these questions.

Through our policy research in Canada and India we observed a few good examples of review processes. To continue our discussion on the case of the Crow Rate policy in Canada, when the policy was eventually overhauled in 1986 in response to several *ad hoc* commissions and studies, a Grain Transportation Agency was created to ensure the freight transport system remained efficient, reliable and effective with the objective of maximizing returns to producers. The new agency was responsible for grain car allocation, system performance monitoring, port coordination and the provision of grain volume forecasts for determining the transportation rate.

In India, for example, the Commission for Agriculture Costs and Prices (CACP) was established to provide recommendations each year to the government for the Minimum Support Price (MSP) for 25 agricultural commodities. The formal review process followed by the CACP is both analytic and deliberative and includes:

- identifying the main issues of relevance for the coming season (short, medium or long term);
- sending out a questionnaire to central ministries, state governments and other organizations related to trade, industry, processors and farmers— both in the cooperative and the private sector—to seek their views on certain issues and factual information on related variables;
- holding separate discussions with these groups, interacting with research and academic institutions, and keeping track of relevant studies and their findings and
- visiting certain areas to make on-the-spot observations and obtain feedback from local organizations.

The review process for a policy pilot as introduced previously provides good guidance for the formal review process. The 2002 study conducted by the UK identified two types of policy pilots:

- *Impact pilots*—tests of the likely effects of new policies, measuring or assessing their early outcomes. They enable evidence of the effects of a policy change to be tested against a genuine counterfactual, such as is provided by the use of control groups in a medical trial.
- *Process pilots*—designed to explore the practicalities of implementing a policy in a particular way or a particular route, assessing what methods of delivery work best or are most cost-effective (UK Cabinet Office, 2003).

The UK study also makes an important point with regard to the critical nature of an independent review:

pilots must be free from real or perceived pressure to deliver 'good news' and be designed to bring out rather than conceal a policy's imperfections. To this end, the Ministers and civil servants most closely involved with the policy should consider distancing themselves from decisions about pilot methods and the dissemination of their findings. (ibid.)

The pilots are conducted as part of the policy design process and result in necessary policy adjustments prior to wider-scale implementation. While we list this here as guidance for conducting a policy pilot, we suggest that this pilot process does, in fact, provide good guidance for a continuous formal policy review process. Given the complex, dynamic and uncertain world in which policy-makers must operate today, a policy, even when implemented on a full scale, is always in a state of pilot testing, and as such, is continually being reviewed from both *impact* and *process* perspectives.

Policy Improvement

There are essentially three types of recommendations that can emerge from the formal review process:

- No policy adjustment is required.
- The policy objective or approach is no longer relevant under the new circumstances and, consequently, the policy should be terminated.
- A policy adjustment is deemed necessary. There are four types of adjustments that can be made

    (a) an adjustment can be made now to make the policy robust across a range of newly anticipated future conditions (without the need for future adjustments);

    (b) an automatic adjustment can be pre-defined now and triggered at an appropriate time in the future (see Chapter 5);

    (c) a system performance indicator is identified to trigger future analysis and deliberation for an anticipated policy adjustment, the precise nature of which cannot yet be determined (manual adjustment—see Chapter 5) or

    (d) further analysis and deliberation is needed to better understand the unanticipated issue and to determine how the policy should be adjusted.

WHEN TO USE FORMAL REVIEW AND CONTINUOUS LEARNING

We advocate that formal review should be an integral part of every policy. It is a process that follows implementation of the policy and, as already noted, is triggered by a preset time interval and also by system performance indicators and stakeholder feedback. With such triggers defined, the review and improvement process is continuous versus *ad hoc*.

Table 9.1 Overview of Formal Policy Review and Continuous Learning

Formal policy review and continuous learning: Regular review, even when the policy is performing well, and the use of well-designed pilots throughout the life of the policy to test assumptions related to performance, can help address emerging issues and trigger important policy adjustments.

Why?	What is it?	How to apply it?	When to use it?
From Holling (1978): • Changes in one variable can have unexpected impacts on variables at the same place but several connections away; • Events at one place can re-emerge as impacts at distant places; • Monitoring the wrong variable can seem to indicate no change even when drastic change is imminent; • Impacts are not necessarily immediate and gradual; they can appear abruptly some time after the event.	The triggers for a review: 1. Pre-defined time interval, that is, once in a year. 2. Monitoring of system performance indicators relating to intended (and unintended) policy outcomes. 3. Stakeholder feedback. 4. Availability of critical new information. Review (the learning): 1. An assessment of current conditions and trends using analytic and deliberative approaches. 2. Forward-looking scenario-based and integrated assessment to detect emerging issues and see the hidden cause–effect relationships. 3. Policy pilot review process.	1. Periodicity dependent on how fast outcomes are anticipated to occur. 2. Threshold values for the indicators trigger review. You likely do not know the cause–effect story, but it is clear that a problem exists or is pending. 3. Strengthen existing processes for reviewing stakeholder feedback. 4. Similar to stakeholder feedback, but source is more scientific. 1. Expert or expert group conducts review based on defined criteria. 2. Expert or expert group conducts review based on defined criteria and considering unanticipated conditions. 3. Phased introduction of policy, to test, evaluate and adjust where necessary, before rolling out at a larger scale (UK Cabinet Office, 2003).	• Formal policy review and continuous learning process are built directly into the design of the policy. They are not *post hoc* additions. • The review processes can be triggered in different ways, as outlined in the first row of this table. • Forward-looking scenario and integrated assessment approaches are used both in the policy design stage and the monitoring and improvement stage.

(*Table 9.1 Continued*)

Why?	What is it?	How to apply it?	When to use it?
	Improvement (the doing):	• Use a deliberative process to identify the necessary revision to the policy objective (see Chapter 4).	• The improvement aspect effectively closes the loop in the policy cycle, between monitoring and policy design.
	• Does the policy objective need to be modified or changed in light of what was learned during the review?	• Scenario analysis and integrated assessment approaches can be leveraged here (see Chapter 3).	
	• Can the policy be adjusted now to ensure its performance in the face of the emerging issue(s)? This is making the policy robust across a range of anticipated conditions.	• Fully- and semi-automatic adjustment mechanisms can be used here (see Chapter 5).	
	• If a robust policy adjustment cannot be identified now, specific indicators should be developed and monitored, and thresholds set to trigger an automatic or manual policy adjustment (Chapter 5).		

While formal review inherently follows a period of policy implementation, the process is crafted (triggers defined, review participants identified, and so on) as part of the design of the policy itself. It is not simply an afterthought.

LINKS WITH OTHER ADAPTIVE POLICY TOOLS

Formal review is similar to automatic adjustment in that it acknowledges that monitoring and remedial measures are integral to complex adaptive systems (Holling, 1978) and that it is necessary to constantly refine interventions through a continual process of variation and selection (Glouberman et al., 2003). However, formal review and continuous learning are distinctly different from automatic adjustment. Automatic adjustment can anticipate what signposts to use and what actions might need to be triggered to keep the policy effective. Formal review, on the other hand, is a mechanism for dealing with unanticipated circumstances and emerging issues.

There is also a subtle, yet fundamental difference between formal review and *ad hoc* review. Both can accomplish the intended result—that being critical policy improvements—but *ad hoc* review relies often on a long period of public debate and analysis before a formal review is triggered. Formal reviews in the context of this chapter are preset processes that occur even if the policy appears to be functioning well and there appears to be no need for review and assessment. This regularly scheduled assessment process is necessary to detect emerging issues and integrate the learning that can impact on the policies performance.

The process of formal review requires that approaches for integrated and forward-looking analysis (Chapter 3) and multi-stakeholder deliberation (Chapter 4) be used for review and identifying necessary policy adjustments. In particular, the approach for formal review is an integral part of the scenario planning approach that is described in Chapter 3. For example, it provides the venue to examine what scenarios are actually becoming reality, facilitating a policy-maker's ability to see the emerging issues that lurk around the corner.

Furthermore, an understanding of complex adaptive systems suggests that the system will often provide clear feedback as to which policies are working and which are not. This is a principle that informed Chapter 8 which dealt with promoting variation in policy approaches in order to build the capacity of a policy to perform better in the face of unanticipated conditions. The formal review and continuous learning process is part of the process of promoting variation in policy approaches—it provides feedback to policy-makers about what is working and what is not.

10 Insights into Implementing Adaptive Policies

Stephan Barg and Stephen Tyler

We suggest in this guide that public policy can be designed to be more adaptive, even to unanticipated conditions, to reduce the risks of policy failure as circumstances change. This is helpful because policies that fail to adapt to key changes in their operating environment will not only fail to achieve their desired objectives, but may actually make things worse. For example, one of the cases examined in this project was the Canadian grain transportation tariff known as the Crow Rate. It started off as a policy tool to support both rail and agricultural development in western Canada. But after decades without revision, it became a barrier to profitability of the railways and this led to poor service for farmers. Had this policy been designed to respond better to changing circumstances, it would not have become inimical to its own goals.

The damage control needed when policies go badly 'off the rails' can be extremely costly and time consuming, both from a political and a professional standpoint. It is much more efficient in the long run to design adaptive features into policies so that less management effort is required and the timing and scope of revisions can be accommodated in the implementation process as a matter of course.

In addition to avoiding difficulties of failure over time, adaptive policy design can also help in gaining policy support. When implications or policy outcomes are uncertain, decision-makers may well prefer to postpone decisions until the issues are better understood. This not only slows decision processes and clogs up policy pipelines, but in some cases, it can exacerbate the problem and further complicate the eventual need for action. However, if decision-makers can be shown policy instruments that will be effective across a range of plausible futures, and can handle anticipated and unanticipated circumstances gracefully, there might be more willingness to make commitments that will unblock policy logjams.

With this chapter, we conclude our guidebook by providing some insights for implementing adaptive policies. As illustrated in Figure 10.1 there are

Figure 10.1 Tasks and Tools for the Adaptive Policy-maker

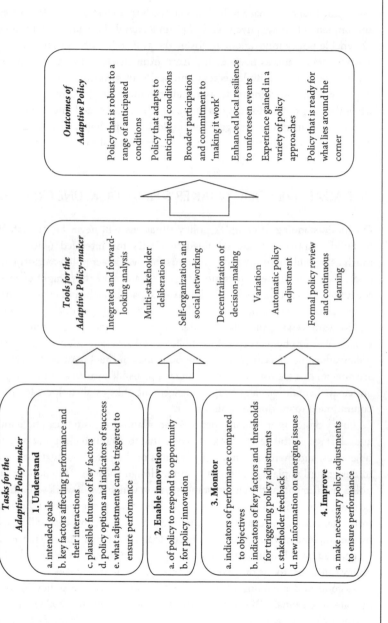

Tasks for the Adaptive Policy-maker

1. Understand

a. intended goals
b. key factors affecting performance and their interactions
c. plausible futures of key factors
d. policy options and indicators of success
e. what adjustments can be triggered to ensure performance

2. Enable innovation

a. of policy to respond to opportunity
b. for policy innovation

3. Monitor

a. indicators of performance compared to objectives
b. indicators of key factors and thresholds for triggering policy adjustments
c. stakeholder feedback
d. new information on emerging issues

4. Improve

a. make necessary policy adjustments to ensure performance

Tools for the Adaptive Policy-maker

Integrated and forward-looking analysis

Multi-stakeholder deliberation

Self-organization and social networking

Decentralization of decision-making

Variation

Automatic policy adjustment

Formal policy review and continuous learning

Outcomes of Adaptive Policy

Policy that is robust to a range of anticipated conditions

Policy that adapts to anticipated conditions

Broader participation and commitment to 'making it work'

Enhanced local resilience to unforeseen events

Experience gained in a variety of policy approaches

Policy that is ready for what lies around the corner

essentially four tasks that a policy-maker needs to undertake in order to create and implement an adaptive policy: (1) understand the policy environment; (2) enable policy innovations to foster the availability of a variety of policy instruments for use as needed, and learn from shared evidence and diverse experience across multiple sectors and scales of government; (3) monitor implementation to compare to assess effectiveness and (4) improve policies when they are not performing as required. These tasks feed into the iterative policy cycle at different stages, and build in adaptability. The seven tools described in this book will help policy-makers undertake these tasks.

THE ADAPTIVE POLICY-MAKER'S FIRST TASK: *UNDERSTAND*

Our understanding of complex policy situations will never be perfect. But to build adaptive policies, we need to clarify the intended objectives as much as possible, identify the key factors that will affect policy performance, understand how these factors are interrelated and how they might evolve in the future. This allows a policy-maker to anticipate how the policy might need to be adjusted over time. In the adaptive policy-maker's toolkit, integrated and forward-looking analysis (Chapter 3) and multi-stakeholder deliberation (Chapter 4) can help create robust policies and also *fully-* and *semi-automatic* policy adjustments (Chapter 5). The outcomes of this broad understanding are policies that are robust across a range of plausible futures and can adapt to anticipated conditions and deeper engagement of key stakeholders to ensure commitment to making the policy work.

Policy design is an iterative process and adaptive measures can be built in at each stage. In the design stage, it is essential to establish clear and practical objectives, and then to identify key features of the policy context that relate to design and implementation. It is in the design stage that the limits to the policy instrument, or the circumstances within which it will work well, should be thought out and planned for. With the objectives and the limits of the policy instrument clear, one can then set the feedback mechanisms that will be used in the implementation phase to ensure that anticipated circumstances are recognized quickly. Part of the design stage is then to anticipate how the new policy can adjust to the range of these anticipated circumstances.

A good understanding of the context within which the policy needs to operate is essential. 'Respect history' Glouberman et al. (2003) say (see Chapter 2). Since almost any policy initiative will overlap or interact with existing policies, these are aspects of the context that bears assessment. These policy overlaps or interactions may cross several different jurisdictional scales, from the global (for example, World Trade Organization regulations) to the local (for example, land use planning). The best way to approach this intimidating range of possibilities is to focus on the specifics of the proposed policy, and analyze the key factors that affect the policy and their inter-linkages, rather than starting with a global list of potentially relevant policies (see Chapter 3). These linkages should be known to local stakeholders, who are aware of what policies affect their actions. The interactions of current policies form an important part of understanding the policy context.

In practical terms, understanding the context can be approached in various ways, but they come back to systematic collection and organization of knowledge. In the research for this volume, for example, case studies as well as interviews with stakeholders were used to gather experience with existing policy instruments. Collecting and analyzing such information provide a way to triangulate evidence of what is working and what is not from the viewpoints of many stakeholders. The academic literature may be a fruitful source of analytical frameworks and reported experience. Focused research efforts such as commissions of inquiry can be extremely helpful, if they were addressing relevant questions. For example, water policy in India and the Crow Rate in Canada have both been the subject of several commissions of inquiry, whose reports bring much information and analysis relevant to defined policy issues together in one place. Indeed, governments may illuminate a complex policy issue by creating such a commission, although this is a time-consuming and costly option. Expert panels, workshops or conferences can be structured to focus attention on relevant knowledge as a shorthand way to gain multiple views.

Another way to gain multiple perspectives is through comparative analysis. In the research for this project, we examined crop insurance in both Canada and India. We also compared the actions taken by multiple institutions operating within the same framework, such as different Conservation Districts in Manitoba or diverse Water Users Associations in India. These comparisons help to identify factors affecting policy design and performance, and would be useful in creating new policy instruments.

In generating contextual knowledge about policy issues, it is important to balance the value of science and of experience in providing evidence: these different forms of knowledge are difficult to compare or to synthesize, but they are complementary.

A good understanding of the issues and policy environment will provide a foundation for setting the objectives of the new policy initiative, be it a revision of an existing instrument or a new instrument. In setting the objectives, multi-stakeholder deliberation (Chapter 4) can help in ensuring that they meet the needs of as many of the stakeholders as possible. Whether the deliberation is done at the community level with the affected people together in the room, or through a representative body, it is useful to get the views and input of people who will be affected. This is especially true where stakeholder support is important to the policy's implementation or functioning.

THE ADAPTIVE POLICY-MAKER'S SECOND TASK: *ENABLE INNOVATION*

As we observed in the case studies, adaptive policies enable diverse responses to opportunities that emerge on the ground, or foster the capacity for innovative local policy implementation. These characteristics of adaptive policy help to address unanticipated circumstances by encouraging learning, innovation and diversity. Enabling these kinds of capacities through policy design is therefore very important in complex, dynamic and uncertain settings. The policy designer should look for opportunities to allow for multiple solutions to be developed and implemented for particular problems, and should also ensure that there are mechanisms to both monitor and share lessons from critical evaluation. These strategies not only manage risk of policy failure by diversification, but also foster the capacity of local organizations to identify and respond quickly to emergent opportunities or threats.

One approach to enabling innovation of this type is to foster self-organization and social networking (Chapter 6). Self-organizing has been described as the process of social interaction around common issues that, from a policy perspective, enables a group to identify and implement innovative solutions. This process of self-organizing has been described as 'social networking', 'building social capital', 'participation' and 'collaboration'. In effect, social networks allow the pooling of knowledge through processes of stakeholder deliberation (factors discussed in Chapters 8 and 4, respectively), but without direct senior government involvement. How do policy-makers foster self-organization without getting explicitly involved in directing it? Promising strategies include removing resource barriers such as information, physical, financial or others; making it easier for such groups to collaborate, copy and share successes; and when developing other policies, recognizing and remaining sensitive to social networks that already exist.

Another tool to foster innovation is decentralization of decision-making (Chapter 7). The rationale for this as an adaptive policy tool is that it puts responsibility closer to those who are most affected by change and enables quicker responses to local priorities. This is particularly relevant for ecosystem management, which must be managed at multiple scales, including the local, because of nested structures and overlapping functions. This points out that the choice of policy area to be decentralized is important: not all issues can be appropriately managed at the local level, and in natural resource issues especially, cross-scale linkages with other levels of government will be important aspects of effective decentralization. It is especially important to consider whether the scale of the activity to be managed by the policy approximates the boundaries of local government units. Governance and accountability are other considerations. The benefits of the approach only adhere if the local decision-making unit is downwardly accountable to local stakeholders. Effective decentralization requires sufficient resources and staff locally to manage and adapt to opportunities as intended.

The effect of these approaches to diverse and decentralized policy implementation is likely to be variation in responses and in adaptive measures. Promoting variation itself encourages resilience, particularly when diverse processes and outcomes can be compared and lessons shared (Chapter 8). Particularly under conditions of high uncertainty, or when policy solutions are not clearly identified, multiple, smaller-scale interventions provide more robust options and spread risks for unanticipated conditions. In this setting, policy-makers can adopt roles as architects of multiple strategies or facilitators of variation in diverse conditions or as learners, comparing outcomes and strengthening successes.

These tools for policy design and implementation build local capacities in assessing and implementing policy. They are often complemented by shared learning mechanisms, such as peer-to-peer exchange, shared experience and critical analysis, and deliberative debate. Deliberative strategies involving multiple stakeholders can be an important part of identifying opportunity and transferring innovation based on these diverse and entrepreneurial local responses. Deliberative mechanisms also build stronger local consensus on what has been learned and on the need for additional action (Chapter 4).

Enabling innovation puts the focus on *learning* through policy development and implementation. In policy domains where we expect turbulence, uncertainty and low predictability, policy-makers will not only need a range of experience but also ways to query, assess and share lessons from that experience. By providing for variable and flexible local responses to policy implementation, these mechanisms enhance local learning and resilience to unforeseen events, increasing responsiveness to key stakeholders in order to build commitment to policy implementation.

THE ADAPTIVE POLICY-MAKER'S THIRD TASK: *MONITOR*

If there is no monitoring of policy implementation in comparison to intended objectives, adaptive policy mechanisms cannot function. While this may seem obvious, most policies do not have regular, built-in monitoring mechanisms. The linkages between policy implementation or impact and policy-makers themselves can be very tenuous, as shown by the case studies for this project. Our case studies were conducted in two large countries, with federal government structures, where there are many policies that are designed at the national level, but delivered at the state or provincial level, or even at a lower level. Formal mechanism to track policy implementation, as well as outcomes, and to communicate this information in a simple format that can be acted upon, are all essential to trigger policy adjustments if necessary.

We describe a tool for integrating monitoring in policy implementation and adjustment in Chapter 5. *Semi- or fully-automatic adjustment* requires identification of the key factors affecting policy performance and an ability to measure indicators that accurately reflect these factors as they evolve over time. Policy adjustments, if required, are then triggered by the values of these indicators as monitored. But given the dynamic and uncertain nature of ecosystems, society and our economy, very few policy adjustments can be pre-defined and triggered at the appropriate time. Dealing with the 'unknown unknowns' will require more than automatic policy adjustment.

Formal policy reviews may be designed into policy implementation using monitoring and triggers (Chapter 9). At a minimum, reviews should be triggered by the passage of a pre-defined time interval to ensure that emerging unanticipated issues can be detected and responses designed. But there are other important triggers such as thresholds (ranges of validity) for indicators of key factors that affect policy performance, targets for policy performance, stakeholder feedback, and the availability of new data and information that challenge the original assumptions underlying policy design and performance.

Monitoring should be selective. There is no need or value to monitoring information that is not informative. So part of monitoring is identifying appropriate indicators that are clear, observable and directly tied to the policy objectives through mechanisms understood from the First Task. Part of the analysis that may be undertaken in trying to anticipate future conditions, for example, may be scenarios of plausible futures (Chapter 3). Monitoring can then trace the key indicators linked to particular scenarios to demonstrate what characteristics of plausible futures are being realized.

It is through systematic policy monitoring and formal policy review that the assumptions about how a policy will perform are tested and assessed. This can also be accomplished through policy pilots of a limited duration. In either case, adaptive policy-makers can make use of integrated and forward-looking analysis and multi-stakeholder deliberation to understand policy performance in complex settings and build consensus on how the policy might be adjusted to achieve its intended objectives.

THE ADAPTIVE POLICY-MAKER'S FOURTH TASK: *IMPROVE*

The adaptive policy cases and tools described in this book illustrate the importance of revising failing policies in the face of new conditions. But demonstrating the need for change does not guarantee that it will take place. Policy-makers often face barriers to policy revision that have little to do with evidence. The more people affected, and the more powerful the entrenched interests, the more difficult a policy change can be to implement. Mechanisms for decentralization (Chapter 7) and for multi-stakeholder deliberation (Chapter 4) provide ways to facilitate policy change. Deliberative mechanisms help to build consensus and identify common values underlying policy. Devolving flexibility for policy change to the local level may make it easier for leaders to build consensus among divergent interests on the need for revisions to meet changing circumstances.

The question of *how* to improve the failing policy takes us back to the same questions as are addressed in designing a new policy. It is necessary to go back, revisit the goals and incorporate adaptive features (among other things) in a redesigned policy. This will complete the policy cycle.

OUTCOMES OF USING ADAPTIVE POLICY TOOLS

How will policy-making and outcomes change if the tools discussed in this guide are used to make policies more adaptive? Referring to Figure 10.1, by using the tools discussed in Chapter 3 (integrated and forward-looking analysis) and Chapter 4 (multi-stakeholder deliberation) policy designers will be considering how sensitive their choices are to plausible alternative futures and multiple interests. Both diverse facts and values can be shared and critically examined using these two approaches. Policy-makers can then address design and implementation decisions with a much broader consideration of the challenges and opportunities they may face. This produces a result that is not optimized for ideal, preferred or even most likely conditions, but is likely to remain robust across a broader range of anticipated circumstances. In using the tools mentioned earlier, policies can be built with the capability to adapt to anticipated conditions as they are experienced over time.

It is the unanticipated circumstances that are more difficult to deal with, of course. But it is possible to prepare for unanticipated conditions by enabling self-organization and social networks (Chapter 6), decentralizing decision-making (Chapter 7) and promoting variation in policy (Chapter 8). Outcomes can be realized such as enhanced local resilience to unforeseen events and a broader participation and commitment to making policy work. Diverse approaches to policy implementation generate a broader response portfolio, so when conditions change, options are already available to address the new context.

In addition to promoting the development of alternative policy solutions, the adoption of recommendations from multi-stakeholder deliberation has the advantage of strengthening local capacity to respond to unforeseen events. It builds civic confidence, recognition of shared values and trust in governance processes. The same advantages hold in the case of self-organization (Chapter 6). Any policy framework that strengthens local social capital will boost adaptive capacity.

The final major outcome of utilizing the adaptive policy approach discussed in this guide is that policy designers will have the tools to recognize promptly when their policies are no longer functioning properly, and have both a broader set of responses at hand, and the experience and knowledge to implement them—to be ready for what lies around the corner. Automatic policy adjustment (Chapter 5) and formal policy review and continuous learning (Chapter 9) are available to policy-makers to help facilitate these outcomes. The result is greater confidence and less reliance on time-consuming crisis management in policy development and revision.

WHEN TO USE ADAPTIVE POLICIES

The seven adaptive policy tools can be used at both the design and implementation stages of the policy cycle (see Figure 2.1). It is often easier to pick and choose from among the most appropriate tools when designing a completely new policy or instrument, but that is an opportunity that may not arise very often. Most policy design work is aimed at making modifications to existing policies, in order to have them better accomplish their objectives, or respond to revised objectives, or address new circumstances. The tools discussed in the preceding chapters are well suited to these tasks, and if implemented regularly, can greatly simplify them.

As we argued in Chapters 1 and 2, the world in which policy must operate is becoming both more complex and dynamic. Adaptive policies provide mechanisms for dealing with the uncertainties involved in any policy decision. But even in complex, interlinked systems, not everything is uncertain. By assembling and structuring knowledge systematically across the various dimensions of a policy issue—social, economic and environmental—policy-makers can design responses to reasonably address a range of anticipated conditions.

We have also seen that policy design and implementation can respond to conditions that were completely unanticipated, through building capacity for flexible responsiveness, social innovation and opportunism. For some policies, features such as deliberation or decentralized decision-making (Chapters 4 and 7), encouraging self-organization and variation (Chapters 6 and 8), or developing continuous learning mechanisms (Chapter 9) can provide opportunities to adapt effectively to the unanticipated. While these characteristics need to be reflected in policy design, they are typically most evident at the implementation stage.

Policy-makers are often confronted by time constraints, by high uncertainty and by political realities. It can be difficult to introduce new policy approaches under these circumstances. But by building on existing knowledge, strengthening monitoring and learning mechanisms, and building evidence for policy change, the risk of failure can be reduced. Policy-makers always want to avoid failure and measure success, but failures can be important sources of learning. Sometimes crisis and failure can provide opportunities to draw lessons and to introduce adaptive approaches to policy formulation.

Policy development is a creative process, not a checklist or a cookbook. The tools discussed in this book can be modified, used independently or in combination. While we have tried to describe the circumstances in which each tool seems most useful, every situation will be different, and appropriate strategies must arise from the contextual details. In each case, we have tried to identify the core elements of the tools that contribute to their effectiveness. These elements may form the seeds for novel approaches. Practitioners may also be aware of other tools not discussed here. We recognize that there is already much experience with some of these tools, and encourage users to modify and adapt the tools themselves, and to share the lessons from such experience in keeping with the learning-oriented theme of this volume.

Our key message is that the tools we present in this guidebook will help policies and policy-makers respond to the uncertain and often unforeseen events that are inevitably faced. By acknowledging uncertainties and using these tools to enhance the adaptive capability of the policy, policy-makers can significantly improve the process of policy design, implementation and revision.

The tools explored in the chapters of this book were derived from real world examples. None of the tools were developed by us—this guide simply brings them together more systematically in the novel context of adaptive policy-making. The adaptive policy approach, therefore, is about looking at existing policy design issues from a different viewpoint, rather than a whole new set of methods. Readers can utilize a similar approach in considering how best to make policies adaptive in their specific situation. By using the principles and tools outlined in this book for adapting to anticipated and unanticipated conditions, policy-makers can adopt a new viewpoint in looking at effective policy experience. Learning from what has worked well in the past, using wide-ranging approaches to thinking about future possible directions and monitoring the success of existing policies against their goals can foster adaptive policies that are both efficient and effective.

Appendix:
Policy Case Study Overviews

CANADA

Crow Rate Grain Transportation Subsidy, p. 134 (Swanson and Venema, 2006)
Manitoba Conservation Districts, p. 135 (Barg and Oborne, 2006)
Manitoba Crop Insurance Program, p. 136 (Swanson and Venema, 2007)
Manitoba Drainage Policy, p. 138 (ibid.)
Saskatchewan Soil Conservation Association's (SSCA) Extension Activities for Minimum Tillage, p. 139 (Roy et al., 2007)
Alberta Irrigation District Program, p. 141 (Swanson et al., 2008)
Canadian Agriculture Income Stabilization Program (CAIS), p. 143 (ibid.)

INDIA

Weather-indexed Insurance in India, p. 144 (Kelkar, 2006)
Agriculture Price Policy in India , p. 145 (Mitra and Sareen, 2006)
Participatory Irrigation Management (PIM) in Maharashtra , p. 147 (Bhadwal, 2008)
National Watershed Development Project for Rainfed Areas (NWDPRA)— Maharashtra Participatory Watershed Management , p. 148 (Tomar and Nair, 2008)
Watershed Development Project in Shifting Cultivation Areas (WDPSCA) in Meghalaya , p. 150 (Tomar and Nair, 2009)
Power Subsidies for Agriculture in Andhra Pradesh, p. 152 (Nair, 2009)

FOR DETAILED VERSIONS OF THESE CASE STUDIES VISIT

http://www.iisd.org/climate/vulnerability/policy_insights.asp
http://www.iisd.org/climate/vulnerability/policy_communities.asp

CROW RATE GRAIN TRANSPORTATION SUBSIDY

Policy Definition and Intent

The Crow Rate w is a regulated tariff policy that subsidized transportation of grain from the Canadian Prairies to ports for export within the country.

Context

The Crow Rate was a long-standing regulated tariff implemented by the Canadian government from 1897 through 1995. It initially supported railway expansion in western Canada at the turn of the last century. A largely unanticipated outcome of the Crow Rate's persistence well into the 20th century was serious under-investment in grain handling and rail transportation infrastructure—shortcomings brought into stark relief when major grain sales to Russia and China in the 1960s almost caused the system to collapse. The failure to consider the effects of rising inflation on the performance of the fixed transportation freight rate would prove to be one of the main culprits. Public pressure eventually catalyzed a complete overhaul of the policy in the form of the Western Grain Transportation Act (WGTA).[1] This new policy would overcome some of the challenges including those related to the static nature of the previous subsidy and would consider a range of input parameters in the determination of the freight rate.

Summary of Adaptive Policy Features of the WGTA

Integrated and forward-looking analysis: Variable costs associated with moving grain were incorporated into the freight rate of the WGTA. This was not done in the original Crow Rate policy. The freight rate under the WGTA would: include the railways' cost of moving grain and intended to cover variable costs plus 20 per cent towards constant costs (five to six times former levels); and be distance-based, designed to allow equal rates for equal distances. As a result, it was more responsive to changes in inflation and transportation costs.

Multi-stakeholder deliberation: The Senior Grain Transportation Committee was a 29-member committee created to advise the Minister of Transport on grain transportation issues. The committee represented different stakeholders from the transportation sector and the Canadian Wheat Board for example.

---

[1] The Western Grain Transportation Act was terminated in 2001 amidst high grain prices and a declining tolerance for an administered rate in a free-market system.

Fully- and semi-automatic policy adjustment: Rates were adjusted each year based on changes to the railway's costs due to changes in inflation.

Formal review and continuous learning: The WGTA incorporated a costing review that was carried out by the National Transportation Agency every four years to take into account productivity and costing changes for grain transport. The Grain Transportation Agency was also formed to ensure that the system stayed efficient, reliable and effective with the objective of maximizing returns to producers.

MANITOBA CONSERVATION DISTRICTS

Policy Definition and Intent

The Canadian province of Manitoba passed the Conservation Districts Act in 1976. It was designed to create partnerships between the provincial government and rural municipalities. The Conservation Districts (CDs) are to implement programmes that meet both local and provincial needs—with a focus on soil conservation and water management. These local organizations are given small budgets with contributions from both provincial and municipal governments, access to government staff expertise and are governed by locally-based boards of directors appointed by the provincial government.

Context

Water management challenges have existed in Manitoba since the province's agricultural settlement period. In response to a rapidly increasing rural agricultural population, drainage was a major focus of municipal and provincial government agencies between 1895 and 1935. In an attempt to understand impacts of upstream water sources, Manitoba conducted several inquiries, beginning in 1918—eventually leading to the formulation of Manitoba's Conservation District Policy in 1976. A watershed-based CD legislation was drafted in 1959 following earlier legislative experiences in Ontario and the United States, but was repealed. Today there are 17 CDs in Manitoba with a mixture of municipal and watershed-based boundaries.

Summary of Adaptive Policy Features

Multi-stakeholder deliberation: CD boards are members of the community and responsive to local issues. Members are selected by elected officials of the rural municipalities within which the district lies and by the provincial government. Proceedings are public and transparent: in some cases hearings on drainage applications are held in the field where the situation can be physically inspected by all concerned.

Enabling self-organization and social networking: The autonomy provided to the CDs under the funding agreement allows them to self-organize around soil and water management issues and make spending decisions based on their on-the-ground needs and changing circumstances. For example, one CD recognized the importance of capping abandoned wells, leading to several other CDs following suit. In another instance, a CD board member identified an ancient Aboriginal ceremonial cite and was able through collaboration with the local Aboriginal community to develop interpretive signage at the site. Both of these are examples of issues not necessarily envisaged at the outset of the CD programme, but which needed to be addressed.

Decentralization of decision-making: CD boards comprise local stakeholders who are able to make spending and programming decisions based on local needs and changing circumstances. While most CDs are based on municipal boundaries, one CD with watershed boundaries was particularly effective at managing the drain licensing process, a task normally managed at the provincial level.

MANITOBA CROP INSURANCE PROGRAM

Policy Definition and Intent

Crop insurance has been prevalent for over half a century in Canada. The policy and operational guidelines for crop insurance approved by provincial Ministers of Agriculture in 1988 stated that the objective of crop insurance is '*to provide insurance protection to farmers on the actuarially sound basis against crop losses caused by natural perils that cannot be reasonably controlled*' (FPCIR, 1989). The Manitoba Crop Insurance Program is the provincial-level implementation mechanism of the Canadian Crop Insurance Act.

Context

It is a consensus legal opinion that constitutional authority for crop insurance in Canada falls largely with the provinces, but it is also acknowledged that the provinces cannot deliver crop insurance on their own given the costs and uncertainty involved. The federal government has mandate to pass legislation governing the release of federal contributions to the provinces and to administer this assistance, as well as helping to ensure coherence among the provincial crop insurance schemes and to review and evaluate these schemes from time to time. The insurance division of the Manitoba Agriculture Services Corporation (MASC) is responsible for administering the crop insurance programme in Manitoba. To ensure the timely issuing of contracts and processing of claims, MASC delivers its services through 19 district offices across Manitoba.

Farm-level interviews revealed that crop insurance was an important mechanism in helping producers cope with unusually wet conditions between 1999 and 2005. In the near term, crop insurance certainly does help farmers cope with damage caused by heavy rainfall, excess moisture, drought and hail. Over the long term, however, exposure to these types of weather events will still exist—and will likely become more frequent in the future due to climate change. Crop insurance is best able to support long-term risk reduction if the payments received are invested in ways that help build resilience to future weather events (for example, reduced tillage, diversification of livestock operations and crops, and maintenance of drainage systems).

Summary of Adaptive Policy Features

Integrated and forward-looking analysis: The average crop yield for determining indemnities reflects an integrated assessment approach—it is determined for different geographic areas having common soil, climate, production and risk characteristics. Within each risk area in the province, base premium rates and yields are adjusted according to soil productivity levels.

Multi-stakeholder deliberation: To help contribute to the effective management of the crop insurance programmes, producers have the option to participate in crop insurance boards, agencies and commissions, and to take part in reviews of the crop insurance programme—to gather multiple perspectives from a range of stakeholders that are impacted by the programme.

Automatic policy adjustment: Two examples of automatic adjustment were introduced into the Manitoba Crop Insurance Program in 2007. These include the Pasture Drought Insurance Pilot Program and the Fall Frost Insurance Pilot Program. Both of these programmes delineate a threshold beyond which insurance payments will be made automatically to the producer. For example, in the pasture drought insurance programme, when rainfall falls below 80 per cent of normal during the growing season, an insurance claim is automatically generated. The Fall Frost Insurance Program is designed in a similar fashion and triggers insurance when temperatures of $-2°C$ or lower are recorded two weeks or more before the average first fall frost date.

Decentralization of decision-making: The Manitoba Crop Insurance Program is implemented via 19 district offices and one coordinating office. Therefore, while crop insurance is given mandate through the Federal Crop Insurance Act, it is administered at the provincial level and implemented via the district offices. This decentralization is, in part, responsible for the positive feedback that the programme receives from producers relating to the utility and responsiveness of the programme in a variety of settings across the province.

Variation: Crop insurance has evolved from a single insurance option pertaining to all crop types and one or two specific types of natural hazards, to a multitude of coverage options for different crop varieties hazards. This evolution has been a response to the diversity of risk faced by farmers in the prairies.

MANITOBA DRAINAGE POLICY

Policy Definition and Intent

The intent of Manitoba's water drainage policies is to enhance the economic viability of Manitoba's agricultural community through the provision of comprehensively planned drainage infrastructure. Drainage infrastructure is defined as that infrastructure which is designed to remove excess rainfall during the growing season, based on the productive capability of the soil and on technical, economic and environmental factors. The maintenance of drains is given a higher priority than reconstruction, while reconstruction is a higher priority than new construction. The policies note that drainage shall be undertaken on a watershed basis, to protect wetland areas, fish habitat and downstream water quality, as well as consider water retention, control and timing of run-off.

Context

The agricultural land base in this Canadian province is approximately 8,100,000 hectares. Close to a quarter of this is made possible through extensive land drainage. This drainage network was constructed to facilitate agricultural development in areas where natural drainage conditions and relatively flat topography maintained large areas of excessively wet soils and significant wetland areas. To cope with excessive moisture conditions, many Manitoba farmers increased their efforts to improve drainage of their lands. Properly maintained drainage infrastructure can increase short- and medium-term capacity to cope with heavy rainfall and excess moisture. However, long-term adaptation is better enabled by investing in changes that mimic the natural landscape. Changes such as managed wetlands and constructing prairie potholes act to retain water in times of drought and regulate water in wetter periods.

Throughout the province, responsibility for most waterways rests with the province. However, at the local level, municipalities and Conservation Districts which have constructed their own drains are responsible for these drainage systems (or this responsibility may have been assigned over time, for example, via CD formation). On-farm drainage is the responsibility of individual agricultural landowners.

Summary of Adaptive Policy Features

Integrated and forward-looking analysis: A benefit-cost analysis approach was taken for determining ultimate drainage feasibility and effectiveness. Soil types, watershed topography, existing drainage and precipitation levels both during and prior to a storm event were all significant factors in the determination (Rigaux and Singh, 1977: 1–12).

Multi-stakeholder deliberation: The Drain Management Program of the Whitemud Conservation District implements a review process based on a concept of building and maintaining solid local partnerships between neighbouring farmers, rural municipalities, provincial regulators and other community stakeholders. Only one project review meeting occurs—in the field, at the actual site of the proposed drain work.

Decentralization of decision-making: In three cases, some or all of the authority for land drainage has been transferred from the municipality to a CD, established among partner municipalities under the Conservation Districts Act. The most effective cases are those in which the boundaries of the CD are watershed based.

Formal policy review and continuous learning: In relation to drainage reconstruction, the policy mandates the provincial government to monitor drainage systems and agricultural productivity, while local governments and CDs have responsibility to monitor local drainage systems and current agricultural needs to ensure effective drainage and assess reconstruction needs.

SASKATCHEWAN SOIL CONSERVATION ASSOCIATION'S (SSCA) EXTENSION ACTIVITIES FOR MINIMUM TILLAGE

Policy Definition and Intent

Minimum and zero-tillage practices are one measure used by farmers in Saskatchewan to adapt to single and multi-year droughts. The practice reduces soil erosion, conserves soil moisture and reduces farm input costs. Federal soil and water conservation policies and programmes including Agriculture and Agri-Food Canada's research and demonstration days on conservation tillage and its Innovation Fund enabled the formation and outreach efforts of the Saskatchewan Soil Conservation Association (SSCA). The SSCA used extension activities including the demonstration of new technologies, communications and workshops to build capacity and help spread the practice of minimum and zero-tillage in Saskatchewan.

Context

During the dry 'dust bowl' years of the 1930s, large amounts of topsoil were lost to wind erosion on the Canadian prairies. A series of soil conservation policies implemented during the 1970s and 1980s encouraged the adoption of minimum and zero-tillage practices by Saskatchewan farmers. The SSCA's extension activities are considered to be a key contributor to the large-scale adoption of conservation tillage agriculture in Saskatchewan for effective soil and water conservation—38 per cent of Saskatchewan producers practiced zero-tillage in 2005.

For a number of years, prairie farmers have adopted reduced or zero-tillage practices to increase soil moisture and quality while also reducing input costs. In some cases, these practices also proved to be beneficial in wetter times, because they allow travel on soggy land. In pursuing this practice, though, it is important to ensure responsible use of herbicides for weed control in order to prevent negative long-term impacts to, for example, groundwater quality, pollinating insects and food quality.

Summary of Adaptive Policy Features

Integrated and forward-looking analysis: The extension activities for the promotion of zero-till farming in Saskatchewan was based on an understanding that the suitability of zero-tillage systems varied according to soil and crop types. This understanding resulted in the adoption of zero-tillage systems in ways that were specific and most suitable to local conditions.

Multi-stakeholder deliberation: The SSCA is governed by a board with representation from farmers, government, NGOs and other related sectors. Decisions are also informed through annual meetings in which members, including farmers, farm industry, conservation agencies, government agencies and academics, can provide inputs to future programming.

Enabling self-organization and social networking: Farmer-to-farmer networking is a programme of the SSCA wherein farmers who are interested in a zero-tillage-related practice are put in touch with a farmer that has experience implementing that practice. This programme allows learning and building of trust between producers and in turn allows for the building of informal learning groups and social capital.

Decentralization of decision-making: The SSCA implements its programmes through localized regional offices and outreach at the community level. This local-level action and implementation translates national soil and water conservation policy (including the Federal National Soil Conservation Program and the Agriculture Green Plan) through provincial support, into local level implementation.

Variation: The SSCA developed a variety of programmes for advancing the use of conservation tillage in Saskatchewan, including: demonstration days showing the multiple values in adopting this practice; promoting related technology through exhibitions and training; allowing peer networking and promoting the multiple co-benefits of conservation tillage, including carbon sequestration and trading benefits.

Formal review and continuous learning: The SSCA's annual conference acts as a formal review and reporting mechanism. Taking into account feedback from its annual conference, the SSCA's motivation for promoting conservation tillage has changed to include opportunities for carbon sequestration and participation in carbon markets.

ALBERTA IRRIGATION DISTRICT PROGRAM

Policy Definition and Intent

Irrigation plays a major role in water management and allocation in Alberta. More than 1.6 million acres of land are irrigated in Alberta, representing two-thirds of all irrigation development in Canada (Alberta Agriculture and Food, 2007). Irrigation accounts for 71 per cent of surface water use in the province. The Irrigation Districts Act (2000) describes an 'Irrigation District' as a corporation that operates in a similar manner to a municipality, with a board of directors responsible for managing the affairs of the district. The main responsibilities of the irrigation districts are to deliver water to irrigation farmers and maintain the irrigation infrastructure. Irrigators within the district have their irrigable acres listed on the district's assessment roll. They pay a flat fee per acre for administration, maintenance and rehabilitation of the irrigation infrastructure, but do not pay for the water itself (Nichol, 2005). The licence granting water allocation rights is owned by the irrigation district, not the individual irrigators.

Context

The St. Mary River Irrigation District (SMRID) has played a key role in helping producers in the vicinity of the town of Coaldale adapt to weather shocks and stresses. A water-sharing agreement brokered in 2001, to deal with drought conditions, is a prime example: the SMRID was an influential player in negotiating, communicating and implementing the mitigation plan, which was an unprecedented sharing of water resources. The SMRID has also been integral to helping producers cope with heavy rains: directly after the rainfall in 2002, the SMRID assisted the county in cutting roads, helped farmers pump water, and worked with Alberta hail and crop insurance providers to recognize flood areas. From a longer-term perspective, they have worked with the counties to make ensure that channels and waterways are set up better to avoid problems of the past.

The role that irrigation itself plays in helping producers adapt to weather stresses presents an interesting discussion. While it is obvious that irrigation does increase the adaptive capacity of producers in the region in the face of drought, it is also the case that exposure to drought in the region still exists, and is likely to increase in the future due to climate change.

Summary of Adaptive Policy Features

Integrated and forward-looking analysis: Representatives from the provincial government formed a technical advisory committee to the irrigation districts and other groups negotiating the 2001 water-sharing agreement. Though not voting members, they attended all meetings to provide information about how priorities might be implemented under a variety of water supply scenarios and about laws and policies (Rush et al., 2004). Through monthly planning sessions, water supply forecasts and water rationing strategies for irrigation and non-irrigation users were formulated. The province then worked with the irrigation districts to calculate estimates of the volume of water that would be available and were also able to calculate values for each farmer using individual on-farm irrigation system data.

Multi-stakeholder deliberation: Each district is run by a board of directors that is elected by farmers owning irrigated land within the district, a structure legislated by the Irrigation Districts Act (2000). The 2001 Water Sharing Agreement provides a specific example of multi-stakeholder deliberation. It brought together a diverse group of stakeholders (irrigation districts, cities and towns, recreational water users, industrial water users) who were able to reach consensus regarding how to equitably share the available water during a drought year. As well, the use of experts from Alberta Environment and Alberta Agriculture Food and Rural Development as a technical advisory committee added another perspective and another level of deliberation. Additionally, with regard to water transfers, an irrigation district is required to hold a public meeting discussing the potential transfer and must hold a plebiscite to gain the approval of at least 50 per cent of the irrigators in the district before the transfer application will go forward to the provincial government.

Automatic policy adjustment: An Irrigation Rehabilitation Program (IRP) was initiated in 1969, and a cost-sharing programme between the provincial government and the 13 irrigation districts was renewed through annual agreements. The aim of the programme is to rehabilitate water conveyance and storage infrastructures. The automatic adjustment mechanism in the policy is in the inter-district funding formula. Fifty per cent of the funds are allocated on the basis of the number of irrigation acres in each district, and 50 per cent of the funds are allocated on the basis of the infrastructure replacement cost of specified infrastructure in each district. Each of these two values will shift within and between irrigation districts from year to year, and thus the policy is able to adjust for changing needs annually.

Enabling self-organization and social networking: In conjunction with other irrigation districts, affected towns and villages, water co-ops and others, the SMRID began developing a disaster communication plan after an extreme rainfall event in 1995. The dry season of 2001 extended the plan to include responses to both drought and flooding, and more extreme rains in 2002 and 2005 began to test the various components of the plan. A district board member noted that 'we now have a much better idea what can happen, and we're much more prepared for it'.

Decentralization of decision-making: The 2001 Water Sharing Agreement emerged from discussions of the Main Canal Advisory Committee made up of managers from the St. Mary River, Taber and Raymond irrigation districts. This committee was already in existence, meeting regularly to discuss the operation of their common irrigation canal. In 2000, the committee started inviting other stakeholders to the table, first expanding to add the four other irrigation districts in the area, and then in the spring of 2001, other affected water users were invited to join the water-sharing group.

CANADIAN AGRICULTURE INCOME STABILIZATION (CAIS) PROGRAMS

Policy Definition and Intent

In Canada, there is a long history of agriculture safety net policies and programmes designed to increase income stability and reduce market risks. Programmes have evolved over recent years to include the National Income Stabilization Account (NISA) in the early 1990s, to its predecessor the Canadian Agriculture Income Stabilization (CAIS) Program introduced in 2003. The CAIS program combined income stabilization assistance and disaster assistance into one comprehensive programme to help producers protect their farming operations from both small and large drops in income. During the preparation of this case study in 2007 and 2008 the third generation of income stabilization mechanisms was being rolled out, which included a suite of business risk management programmes.

Context

Both the CAIS and the previous NISA programmes were frequently cited by agriculture producers as helping them cope with weather-related stresses. The CAIS program has recently undergone a major redesign in response to negative feedback from farmers and other experts. The general attitude of producers was that the CAIS program was an overly complicated and difficult programme to use. Specific comments were that it was poorly designed, that there was high costs associated with submitting claims through the programme, and it always seemed to be changing. In the words of one producer, it is understandable that it was so complex, because how can a programme be designed to suit the needs of over 100,000 producers nationwide.

Cited in the following are adaptive policy features observed in the three generations of income stabilization programmes in Canada, and as is specifically implemented in the province of Alberta.

Summary of Adaptive Policy Features

Multi-stakeholder deliberation: For the new business risk management suite of programmes, national stakeholder consultations were held with over 3,000 producers and processors to understand what the sector requires to effectively manage risk.

Automatic policy adjustment: Under the NISA programme withdrawals were triggered when gross margins fell below a three-year average (gross margin trigger) or when family income fell below a minimum family income level (minimum income trigger).

Decentralization of decision-making: In 1995 Alberta withdrew from the federal NISA programme based on concerns that it was not meeting the needs of Albertan producers and was inefficient. Alberta began extensive consultations with producers across Alberta, leading to the creation of the Farm Income Disaster Program (FIDP) tailored to the needs of the province. FIDP provided income support to Albertan producers experiencing, for reasons beyond their control, an extreme reduction in farm income. The programme was designed to supplement the net income of farmers, regardless of the commodity, when the current year net income fell below the 70 per cent of the average for the preceding five years.

Promoting variation: Under the new income stabilization programme, a suite of programmes are being developed to compliment one another and manage risk: *AgriInvest*—provides coverage for small income declines and allows for investments that help mitigate risks or improve market income; *AgriStability*—provides support when a producer experiences larger farm income losses; *AgriRecovery*—provides a coordinated process for federal, provincial and territorial governments to respond rapidly when disasters strike, filling gaps not covered by existing programmes and *AgriInsurance*—an existing programme which includes insurance against production losses for specified perils (weather, pests, disease).

WEATHER-INDEXED INSURANCE IN INDIA

Policy Definition and Intent

Weather-indexed insurance is linked to the underlying weather risk defined as an index based on weather data (for example, rainfall), rather than crop yield loss. As the index is objectively measured and is the same for all farmers, the problem of adverse selection is minimized, the need to draw up and monitor individual contracts is avoided and the administration costs are reduced.

Context

Various pilot schemes and delivery models are being explored in India. For example, ICICI Lombard General Insurance Company, with support from the World Bank and International Finance Corporation, conceptualized and launched a pilot rainfall insurance scheme in Mahabubnagar, Andhra Pradesh in July 2003. The district had previously experienced three consecutive droughts. The scheme was implemented through the Krishi Bima Samruddhi (KBS) local area bank of BASIX. KBS Bank bought a bulk insurance policy from ICICI Lombard and sold around 250 individual policies to groundnut and castor farmers. The index capped rainfall per sub-period at 200 mm, and weighted critical periods for plant growth more heavily than others.

Summary of Adaptive Policy Features

Automatic policy adjustment: Unlike traditional crop insurance where settling a claim can take up to a year, private weather insurance contracts offer quick payouts triggered by independently-monitored weather indices (rather than farm loss sampling). This improves recovery times, thereby enhancing coping capacity. The automatic adjustment feature provides a simple mechanism for managing insurer risk and determining farmer eligibility for benefit payments, while also passing along incentives for farmers to adjust to long-term change by providing appropriate signals calculated on the basis of actuarial risk.

Multi-stakeholder deliberation: Another element of adaptability in the implementation of weather-indexed insurance stems from the engagement of local micro-finance institutions (MFIs) that have already established a presence and working relationships with agricultural communities. The experiences of MFIs in delivering insurance to the rural poor have revealed the critical importance of product design, communication and marketing approach. Self-help groups (SHGs) and e-*choupals* (village Internet kiosks) have been innovatively used to create awareness and trust in insurance, along with providing information about prices, cropping practices and product and providing loans or agricultural input.

Decentralization of decision-making: The delivery of weather insurance through local micro-finance institutions suggests the importance of two-way communication channels in fostering adaptive policy design by building in feedback mechanisms to respond to changing client needs or other conditions.

Formal review and continuous learning: Weather-indexed insurance was implemented on a pilot basis for various crops and locations by trying out different types of delivery models. The use of pilots has been suggested as a feature of an adaptive, learning-oriented policy system. ICICI Lombard and BASIX have reported that this pilot experience was valuable to better understand risk patterns and the potential for commercial expansion. It was also an opportunity to create awareness among farmers, build trust through timely payouts and improve the product design in response to customer feedback.

AGRICULTURE PRICE POLICY IN INDIA

Policy Definition and Intent

An Agriculture Price Policy was initiated by the Government of India to provide protection to agricultural producers against any sharp drop in farm prices. If there is a good harvest and market prices tend to dip, the government guarantees a minimum support price (MSP) or floor price to farmers, which covers not only the cost of production, but also ensures a reasonable profit margin for the producers.

Context

Widespread promotion of Green Revolution technologies during the 1960s increased agricultural yields in India for some crops. Adoption of the new technologies involved the use of non-conventional input and investments on the part of the farmers. This made it necessary to create a stable and profitable environment for farmers adopting the new seeds.

The Agricultural Prices Commission (APC) was set up in January 1965 to advise the government on price policy of major agricultural commodities. The objective was to give due regard to the interests of the producer and the consumer, while keeping in perspective the overall needs of the economy. Since March 1985, the commission has been known as Commission for Agricultural Costs and Prices (CACP). The commission consists of a chairman, a member secretary, two official members and three non-official members. The non-official members are representatives of the farming community. They are usually persons with considerable field experience and an active association with the farming community.

Some features of the Agriculture Price Policy may be ecologically maladaptive to future climate impacts. For instance, in the state of Punjab, price incentives that did not internalize natural resource costs resulted in cultivators getting locked into a highly irrigation-intensive cropping pattern, which is drastically depleting already limited groundwater supplies.

Summary of Adaptive Policy Features

Integrated and forward-looking analysis: The CACP takes into account important factors, such as cost of production, changes in input prices and trends in market prices, in announcing the MSP each year. The CACP carries out state-specific analyses for the cost of production in respect of various commodities. This is done through consultations with the state governments. After a meeting of the state chief ministers, the MSP/procurement prices are declared. Cost of production for the same crops varies between regions, across farms within the same region and for different producers.

Multi-stakeholder deliberation: The CACP follows a definite process to arrive at recommendations regarding MSPs. First, the commission identifies the main issues of relevance for the ensuing season (short, medium or long turn). Second, the commission sends a questionnaire to central ministries, state governments and other organizations related to trade, industry, processors and farmers, both in the cooperative and the private sector. Furthermore, it seeks their views on certain issues and factual information on related variables. Next, the commission holds separate discussions with the state governments, central ministries/departments and other organizations. The commission also interacts with research and academic institutions and keeps track of relevant studies and their findings. Finally, the commission visits certain areas to make on-the-spot observations and obtain feedback from local-level organizations and farmers.

Formal review and continuous learning: The MSP is announced each year and is fixed after taking into account the recommendations of the CACP.

PARTICIPATORY IRRIGATION MANAGEMENT (PIM) IN MAHARASHTRA

Policy Definition and Intent

Following a phase of institutional strengthening in 2001 the government made farmers participation in irrigation management obligatory and enacted the Maharashtra Management of Irrigation System by Farmers Act, 2005. About 1,329 Water Users Associations (WUAs) have been formed till date that cover an area of 0.49 million hectares of land.

The state monitors the formation of and devolution of powers. WUAs or farmer cooperatives manage the distribution of irrigation water along canal networks. The legal framework for participatory irrigation management (PIM) outlines the creation of farmers' organizations at different levels of the irrigation systems, including:

- WUAs—covers a group of outlets in a minor addressing such aspects as preparation of irrigation schedules at the end of each cropping season, carry out maintenance of system, regulate use of water, promote efficiency in water use, collect taxes, monitor water flows, resolve local disputes, among other tasks;
- Distributary Committees—comprising of five or more WUAs and
- Project Committees—apex committee of an irrigation system and presidents of the distributary committees in the project area.

Context

The Government of Maharashtra initiated the formation of WUAs in the 1990s following the emphasis laid out in the National Water Policy of 1987. The PIM was developed to create ownership of water resources and irrigation systems at the user level; encourage the need for effective water resource management; improve service deliveries through better operation and maintenance and achieve optimum utilization of available resources in an equitable manner; increase production per unit of water where water is scarce and production per unit of land where water is adequate; and facilitate users in crop choices and other agricultural practices based on water allocations (GoI, 2002).

Summary of Adaptive Policy Features

Enabling self-organization and social networking: The policy instrument encourages the formation of WUAs and provides the legal support for these entities to administer their activities. NGOs have been encouraged to build capacity of these institutions through training and other modes to undertake core activities.

Formal review and continuous learning: The mid-term appraisal of India's Tenth Five-Year Plan (2002–07) reviewed the progress of takeover of irrigation systems by WUAs. It found that there were about 55,000 WUAs covering 10 million hectares, and aimed to increase this 8–10 times in order to cover all irrigated area. It has called for empowerment of WUAs to set tariffs and retain a part of it, understanding barriers and simultaneously rehabilitating them so that they are in a position to invest in infrastructure repairs and improvement. The situation was again reviewed more recently in formulating the approach for the Eleventh Five-Year Plan (2007–11). Greater emphasis has been given to equitable distribution and empowerment of democratically organized WUAs. The Maharashtra State Water Policy also has a clause for review every five years.

Decentralization of decision-making: PIM recognizes the roles of different institutions in the execution of the policy instrument, but bases the implementation of the policy instrument through local feedback and knowledge sharing.

NATIONAL WATERSHED DEVELOPMENT PROJECT FOR RAINFED AREAS (NWDPRA)—MAHARASHTRA PARTICIPATORY WATERSHED MANAGEMENT

Policy Definition and Intent

The objectives of the NWDPRA project are as follows:

- enhancement of agricultural productivity and production in a sustainable manner;
- restoration of ecological balance in the degraded and fragile rainfed ecosystems by greening these areas through appropriate mix of trees, shrubs and grasses;
- reduction in regional disparity between irrigated and rainfed areas and
- creation of sustained employment opportunities for the rural poor.

In Maharashtra, the NDWPRA project continued in India's Ninth Five-Year Plan, when it was considerably restructured. Greater emphasis was placed on decentralization and community participation. In the Tenth Five-Year Plan, the state of Maharashtra continued to implement the NWDPRA scheme with a participatory approach. NWDPRA scheme has been extended to 433 micro-watersheds across 33 districts with targeted treatment area of 2.03 lakh hectares for implementation.

Context

In India, watershed development was not originally conceived as a vehicle for rural development. The original concept of watershed management was management of resources in medium or large river valleys in order to prevent rapid run-off water and slow down the rate of siltation of reservoirs and limit the incidence of potentially damaging flash floods (Smith, 1998). However, long-term experiments by a number of research organizations in India in the 1970s and 1980s confirmed that the introduction of appropriate physical barriers to soil and water flows, together with re-vegetation, could generate considerable increase in resource productivity. These in turn stimulated the formulation of a number of government projects, schemes and programmes in support of micro watershed development (Jensen et al., 1996). There has been strong growth in both government and non-government institutional capacity to implement watershed development projects. This has been further strengthened by integrating the participatory approaches in watershed management. Within semi-arid areas, one may find co-existing programmes under the auspices of several different agencies, including Ministry of Agriculture and Cooperation, Ministry of Rural Development, Ministry of Environment and Forests as well as various bilateral and multilateral donors.

Summary of Adaptive Policy Features

Enabling self-organization and social networking: Under the NWDPRA four types of groups are to be organized at the village level namely: SHGs are a voluntary group of people who come together to take up group activities on a self-help basis for their benefit; User Groups include members who are land owners within the identified watershed area; the Watershed Association (WA) will be the General Body comprising all members of the Watershed Community who agree to participate in the watershed development project and would approve the Strategic Plan and Annual Action Plan as well as carry out review of progress during implementation phase; the Watershed Committee (WC) shall act as the executive body of the WA and carry out the day-to-day activities of the watershed development project subject to overall supervision and control of the Watershed Association.

Formal review and continuous learning: The policy is reviewed continuously by the Government of India and the necessary modifications are incorporated during the five-year plans. The Planning Commission, Government of India, constituted a Working Group on 'Watershed Development, Rainfed Farming and Natural Resources Management' for the formulation of the Tenth Five-Year Plan (2002–07). This included review of various ongoing schemes and projects in the sphere of natural resource management, particularly the programmes based on the watershed development approach under the Ministries of Agriculture, Rural Development and Environment & Forests. In order to get a systematic feedback and analysis of the schemes of the three concerned ministries, three sub-groups were constituted, one for each of the three ministries. These sub-groups were entrusted with the responsibility of examining the existing projects, identifying their strengths, weaknesses, constraints and bottlenecks in their implementation and for suggesting appropriate measures for the Tenth Five-Year Plan, so as to achieve the objective of sustainable development and utilization of natural resources. They were also asked to review the progress under the ongoing schemes and suggest proposals for the Tenth Five-Year Plan, based on the experiences gained as well as the objectives to be achieved.

Decentralization of decision-making: Under the revised guidelines, contractors were eliminated from the process to enable individual farmers to implement treatments with the financial and technical assistance on private holdings and village associations/ beneficiary groups to implement community works. These modifications in the policy incorporate an element of subsidiarity which would help farmers adapt better to years of low rainfall by conserving water. The guidelines provided that:

> ... in the project implementation, the physical treatments would be decided in active consultations with individual farmers and village communities. In fact the current farming systems and practices should be thoroughly analyzed and farmers' experiences and skills should be given due emphasis. The project staff may have to learn a lot from the village community and unlearn some of their orthodox views and theoretical presumptions about people's capabilities. Thus, in the ultimate analysis science and technology from research institutions, technical and managerial know-how of the project staff and accumulated experience of the village community should be symbiotically integrated to finalize the choice of treatments in the watersheds.
>
> GoI (1994)

WATERSHED DEVELOPMENT PROJECT IN SHIFTING CULTIVATION AREAS (WDPSCA) IN MEGHALAYA

Policy Definition and Intent

The Watershed Development Project in Shifting Cultivation Areas (WDPSCA) scheme is taken up on a watershed basis for treatment of arable and non-arable lands affected by shifting cultivation and to provide alternative farming methods to the farmers. It is implemented through the Ministry of Agriculture and Cooperation, Government of India as a Special Central Assistance to the State Plan Programme for the benefit of 'jhumia' (shifting cultivation) families who are living below the poverty line. The main objectives of the scheme are as follows:

- Protect and develop the hill slopes of jhum areas through different soil and water conservation measures on a watershed basis and to reduce further land degradation process.

- Encourage and assist the jhumia families to develop jhum land for productive use with improved cultivation and suitable package of practices leading to settled cultivation practices.
- Improve the socio-economic status of jhumia families through household/land-based activities.
- Mitigate the ill effects of shifting cultivation by introducing appropriate water management as per capability and improved technologies.
- Skill development through a training and visit (T&V) component.

As a whole the focus is on natural resource management, economic enhancement, leading to poverty alleviation and eco-friendly living.

Context

In Meghalaya about 530 square kilometres is under shifting cultivation. As the land and water resources are depleting in the state, the government has taken up various conservation measures and developmental programmes in arable and non-arable lands. The jhum control programme is one of the schemes aimed at combating further deterioration of fertile topsoil. The main thrust of the scheme is to provide an effective supporting base for permanent settlement of the communities engaged in jhum cultivation.

Summary of Adaptive Policy Features

Decentralization of decision-making: The organizational structure for implementation of the WDPSCA scheme involves the following set-up at the national, state and local level: the National watershed committee chaired by Secretary, Department of Agriculture & Cooperation; the National Coordination by Natural Resource Management Division, Department of Agriculture & Cooperation; State Level Watershed Steering Committee, chaired by Chief Secretary; State Nodal Department; the District Watershed Development Committee; the Watershed Association, Watershed Committee, and self-help groups and User Group.

Formal review and continuous learning: There is periodical review of progress during the implementation phase at the district, state and national level under India's national Five-Year Plan process. A system of concurrent evaluation has also evolved through internal as well as external agencies. In such evaluation studies, a critical assessment is made of the relevance of technological content, involvement of people in the programme, gender equity and equity for poor farmers, facilitation of group action, and so on. On completion of the project, an impact evaluation is undertaken by external agencies.

POWER SUBSIDIES FOR AGRICULTURE IN ANDHRA PRADESH

Policy Definition and Intent

Policies for power subsidies for agriculture have been unevenly distributed among states in India, with Andhra Pradesh being among the states receiving highest subsidies per hectare of cropped land. With the coming in power of a new political party in 2004, 100 per cent free power for agriculture was announced and implemented in Andhra Pradesh.

Context

Communities within Katherapalli village (Chittoor district) and Neramatla village (Anantapur district) were found to be able to cope with climatic shocks and stresses and associated risks to agricultural yields. This was primarily owing to the subsidized rates of power for agriculture for irrigation, thereby allowing for cultivation of crops throughout the year. Across the country, having flat rates on power consumption in agriculture has resulted in over-use of groundwater resources.

A few examples of where adaptive policy features would have benefited the subsidy are highlighted in the following sections.

Summary of Potential Adaptive Policy Features

Integrated and forward-looking assessment: A few months after the announcement of the free power policy, there was a reported rise in number of un-authorized connections. Furthermore, large farmers that make up only 5–6 per cent of the total farming community, account for over 30 per cent of the total agricultural energy consumption for their large farms, horticultural lands and so on. The blanket free power policy hence benefited these large farmers who could now enhance the capacities of their pump sets (PRAYAS, 2004). The subsidy would have benefited from an integrated assessment to detect the varied use of the policy. Consequently, the subsidy had to be revised within a year of coming into existence.

Formal review and continuous learning: Strong oppositions to the free power for agriculture policy voiced the ecological implications in the form of over-extraction of groundwater that is already dwindling in several regions (PRAYAS, 2004). However, there is no formal mechanism or framework to review the policy periodically and building lessons from the ground.

Consolidated Bibliography

Acheson, J.M. (2006). 'Institutional failure in resource management', *Annual Review of Anthropology*, 35: 117–34.

Agarwal, A. and S. Narian (1989). *Towards green villages: A strategy for environmentally sound and participatory rural development*. New Delhi: Centre for Science and Development.

Agriculture and Agri-Food Canada (AAFC) (2007). 'Replacing the Canadian Agricultural Income Stabilization (CAIS) program'. Retrieved 30 January 2008 from http://www.agr. gc.ca/caisprogram/factsheets/faq_caisreplace.html.

———. (2008). '$8.8M for Alberta Water Projects'. Press Release. Retrieved 20 March 2008 from http://news.gc.ca/web/view/en/index.jsp?articleid=386569&categoryid=16.

Alberta Agriculture and Food (2007). *Irrigation in Alberta: Facts and Figures for the Year 2006*. Resource Sciences Branch, Agriculture Stewardship Division.

Arnstein, S. (1969). 'A ladder of citizen participation', *Journal of the American Planning Association*, 35(4): 216–24.

Axelrod, R. and M.D. Cohen (2000). *Harnessing complexity: Organizational implications of a scientific frontier.* New York: Basic Books.

Bankes, S.C. (2002). 'Tools and techniques for developing policies for complex and uncertain systems', *PNAS: Proceedings of the National Academy of Sciences*, 99(3): 7263–66. Retrieved October 2006 from www.pnas.org/cgi/content/full/99/suppl_3/7263.

Barg, S. and B. Oborne (2006). 'Adaptive policy case study: Analysis of Manitoba's conservation district policy', in *Designing policies in a world of uncertainty, change and surprise*. The International Institute for Sustainable Development and The Energy and Resources Institute. Retrieved June 2008 from www.iisd.org/climate/vulnerability/policy_insights.asp.

Berkes, F. (2007). 'Understanding uncertainty and reducing vulnerability: Lessons from resilience thinking', *Natural Hazards*, 41(2): 283–95.

Berkes, F., J. Colding and C. Folke (2003). *Navigating social-ecological systems: Building resilience for complexity and change.* Cambridge, UK: Cambridge University Press.

Bhadwal, S. (2008). *Understanding adaptive policy mechanisms through participatory irrigation management in Maharashtra, India.* The Energy and Resources Institute. Retrieved July 2008 from www.iisd.org/climate/vulnerability/policy_communities.asp.

Busenberg, G.J. (2001). 'Learning in organizations and public policy', *Journal of Public Policy* 21(2): 173–89.

Cash, D.W., W. Adger, F. Berkes, P. Garden, L. Lebel, P. Olsson et al. (2006). 'Scale and cross-scale dynamics: Governance and information in a multilevel world', *Ecology and Society*, 11(2): 8.

Chambers, S. (2003). 'Deliberative democratic theory', *Annual Review of Political Science*, 6: 307–26.

Cheema, G.S. and D.A. Rondinelli (2007). *Decentralizing governance: Emerging concepts and practices.* Washington, DC: Brookings Institution Press.

Curtis, A., B. Shindler and A. Wright (2002). 'Sustaining local watershed initiatives: Lessons from landcare and watershed councils', *Journal of the American Water Resources Association*, 38(5): 1207–16.

Curtis, A. and M. Van Nouhuys (1999). 'Landcare participation in Australia: The volunteer perspective', *Sustainable Development*, 7(2): 98–111.

Daniels, S. and G. Walker (1996). 'Collaborative learning: Improving public deliberation in ecosystem-based management', *Environmental Impact Assessment Review*, 16(2): 71–102.

Delli Carpini, M., F.L. Cook and L.R. Jacobs (2004). 'Public deliberation, discursive participation and citizen engagement: A review of the empirical literature', *Annual Review of Political Science*, 7: 315–44.

Dewey, J. (1927). *The public and its problems*. New York: Holt and Company.

Doss, C., J. McPeak and C. Barrett (2006). 'Interpersonal, intertemporal and spatial variation in risk perceptions: Evidence from east Africa', Centre Discussion Paper No. 948. New Haven, CT: Economic Growth Center, Yale University.

Dungan, P. and S. Murphy (1995). 'Unemployment insurance macroeconomic stabilization'. Retrieved September 2005 from Human Resources Development Canada, http://www.hrsdc.gc.ca/en/cs/sp/hrsdc/edd/reports/1995-000309/page00.shtml.

Economic Survey Board (1940). *Crop insurance in Manitoba*. A report on the feasibility and practicability of crop insurance in Manitoba. Prepared by the Economic Survey Board, Province of Manitoba, February 1940. Available at the Manitoba Legislative Library, Canada.

Ellerman, D. (2004). 'Parallel experimentation: A basic scheme for dynamic efficiency'. Retrieved June 2008 from http://ssrn.com/abstract=549963.

Ellis, F. (1999). 'Rural livelihood diversity in developing countries: Evidence and policy implications', *Natural Resource Perspectives*, No. 40 (April), Overseas Development Institute (ODI), United Kingdom.

———. (2000). *Rural livelihoods and diversification in developing countries*. Oxford: Oxford University Press.

Fabricius, C., C. Folke, G. Cundill and L. Schultz (2007). 'Powerless spectators, coping actors, and adaptive co-managers: A synthesis of the role of communities in ecosystem management', *Ecology and Society*, 12(1). Retrieved June 2008 from www.ecologyandsociety.org/vol12/iss1/art29/.

Folke, C., S. Carpenter, T. Elmqvist, L. Gunderson, C.S. Holling, B. Walker et al. (2002). 'Resilience and sustainable development: Building adaptive capacity in a world of transformations', ICSU Series on Science for Sustainable Development, No. 3. Scientific Background Paper commissioned by the Environmental Advisory Council of the Swedish Government in preparation for the World Summit on Sustainable Development. Paris: ICSU.

Forester, J. (1999). *The deliberative practitioner: Encouraging participatory planning processes*. Cambridge, MA: MIT Press.

FPCIR (1989). *Federal-Provincial Crop Insurance Review: Discussion paper*. Federal-Provincial Crop Insurance Review Committee.

Gadgil, M. and R. Guha (1992). *This fissured land: An ecological history of India*. New Delhi: Oxford University Press.

Global Environment Outlook (GEO) (1997, 1999, 2002, 2008). Global Environment Outlook reports. United Nations Environment Programme, Division of Early Warning and Assessment. Retrieved April 2008 from http://unep.org/GEO.

Glouberman, S. (2007). *Meeting report for Phase III of the teaching as a profession initiative: Schooling for tomorrow project*. Ontario: Instruction and Leadership Development Division, Ontario Ministry of Education (Canada).

Glouberman, S., M. Gemar, P. Campsie, G. Miller, J. Armstrong, C. Newman et al. (2006). 'A framework for improving health in cities: A discussion paper', *Journal of Urban Health*, 83(2), 325–38.

Glouberman, S., P. Campsie, M. Gemar and G. Miller (2003). *A toolbox for improving health in cities*. Ottawa, Canada: Caledon Institute for Social Policy.

Government of Canada (2006). 'Review finds Canada Pension Plan is financially sound'. Retrieved May 2008 from Department of Finance, Government of Canada, www.fin.gc.ca/news06/06-026e.html.

GoI (Government of India) (1994). *Guidelines for watershed development*. Departments of Wasteland Development, Ministry of Rural Development, GoI, New Delhi.

——— (2002). *National Water Policy 2002*. Government of India, Ministry of Water Resources. Retrieved June 2008 from http://wrmin.nic.in/index1.asp?linkid=201& langid=1.

Government of Maharashtra (2005). 'Maharashtra Act No. XXIII of 2005 to provide for management of irrigation systems by farmers'. Retrieved March 2007 from http://www.ielrc.org/content/e0505.pdf.

Gunderson, L.H. and C.H. Holling (2003). *Panarchy: Understanding transformations in human and natural systems*. Washington, DC: Island Press.

Gunderson, L.H., C.S. Holling and S.S Light (1995). *Barriers and bridges to the renewal of ecosystems and institutions*. New York: Columbia University Press.

Gunderson, L.H. and Jr. L. Pritchard (eds) (2002). *Resilience and the behavior of large-scale systems*. Washington, DC: Island Press.

Gupta, S., D.A. Tirpak, N. Burger, J. Gupta, N. Höhne, A.I. Boncheva et al. (2007). 'Policies, instruments and co-operative arrangements', in B. Metz, O.R. Davidson, P.R. Bosch, R. Dave and L.A. Meyer (eds), *Climate change 2007: Mitigation*, pp. 745–807. A contribution of Working Group III to the Fourth Assessment Report of the Intergovernmental Panel on Climate Change (IPCC). Cambridge, UK: Cambridge University Press.

Haas, P.M. (1992). 'Epistemic communities and international policy coordination', *International Organization*, 46(1): 1–35.

Hanumantha Rao, C.H. (2000). 'Watershed development in India: Recent experiences and emerging issues', *Economic and Political Weekly*, XXXV(45): 3943–47.

Hazell, P. (2003). 'The green revolution', in J. Mokyr (ed.), *Oxford encyclopedia of economic history*. Oxford: Oxford University Press.

Helliwell, J. (2001). 'Social capital—Editorial', *ISUMA—Canadian Journal of Policy Research*, 2 (1), 6–7.

Holling, C.S. (1978). *Adaptive environmental assessment and management*. New York: John Wiley and Sons.

———. (2001). 'Understanding the complexity of economic, ecological and social systems', *Ecosystems*, 4(5): 390–405.

Homer-Dixon, T. (2006). *The upside of down: Catastophe, creativity and the renewal of civilization*. Toronto: Random House of Canada Ltd.

IISD (1993). 'Criteria for Great Plains sustainability'. Retrieved June 2008 from the International Institute for Sustainable Development, www.iisd.org/agri/GPcriteria.htm.

———. (2002). *Seven questions to sustainability: How to assess the contribution of mining and minerals activities*. Mining, Minerals and Sustainable Development (MMSD) Project—North America. Retrieved June 2008 from the International Institute for Sustainable Development, www.iisd.org/pdf/2002/mmsd_sevenquestions.pdf.

Innes, A.D., P.D. Campion and F.E. Griffiths (2005). 'Complex consultations and the "edge of chaos"', *The British Journal of General Practice*, 55(510): 47–52.

Irrigation Districts Act (2000). *Agriculture and Rural Development*. Government of Alberta, Canada. Retrieved July 2008 from http://www1.agric.gov.ab.ca/$department/deptdocs.nsf/all/acts6120.

Irrigation Water Management Study Committee (IWMSC). (2002). *South Saskatchewan River Basin (SSRB): Irrigation in the 21st century—Vol. 1 summary report*. Lethbridge, Alberta: Alberta Irrigation Projects Association.

Jäger, J., D. Rothman, C. Anastasi, S. Kartha and P. van Notten (2008). 'Training Module 6—Scenario development and analysis', in L. Pintér, J. Chenje and D. Swanson (eds), *IEA training manual: A training manual on integrated environmental assessment and reporting.* United Nations Environment Programme and the International Institute for Sustainable Development. Retrieved December 2008 from http://gcp.aspen.grida.no/training/manual.

Jensen, J., S. Seth, T. Sawney and P. Kumar (1996). 'Watershed development: Proceedings of Danida's internal workshop on watershed development', Watershed Development Coordination Unit, Danida, New Delhi.

Joshi, P.K., L. Tewari, A.K. Jha and R.L. Shiyani (2000). *Meta analysis to assess impact of watershed. Proceedings workshop on institutions for greater impact technologies.* New Delhi, India: National Centre for Agriculture Economics and Policy Research (NCAP).

Joshi, P.K., V. Pangare, B. Shiferaw, S.P. Wani, J. Bouma and C.A. Scott (2004). *Socio-economic and policy research on watershed management in India: Synthesis of past experiences and needs for future research.* Global Theme on Agro-ecosystem, Report No. 7, International Crops Research Institute for Semi-arid Tropics, Patancheru, India.

Joy, K.J., Suhas Parnjpe, Amita Shah, Shrinivas Badigar et al. (2005). 'Scaling up of watershed development projects in India: Learning from first generation projects', Fourth IWMI-Tata Annual Partners Meet, International Water Management Institute, Anand, India. pp. 133–34.

Kauffman, S. (1993). *The origins of order.* New York: Oxford University Press.

Kay, J., H. Regier, M. Boyle and G. Francis (1999). An ecosystem approach for sustainability: Addressing the challenge of complexity. *Futures*, 3(7): 721–42.

Kelkar, U. (2006). 'Adaptive policy case study: Weather indexed insurance for agriculture in India. Designing policies in a world of uncertainty, change and surprise', in *Adaptive policymaking for water resources and agriculture in the face of climate change.* The International Institute for Sustainable Development and The Energy and Resources Institute. Retrieved June 2008 from www.iisd.org/climate/vulnerability/policy_insights.asp.

Kemper, K.E., W. Blomquist and A. Dinar (2007). *Integrated river basin management through decentralization.* Berlin Heidelberg: Springer-Verlag.

Kerr, J., G. Pangare and V. Pangare (2004). *Watershed development projects in India: An evaluation.* Research Report 127. Washington, DC: International Food Policy Research Institute.

Koontz, T.M. (2006). 'Collaboration for sustainability? A framework for analyzing government impacts in collaborative-environmental management', *Sustainability: Science, Practice and Policy*, 2(1): 15–24.

Koontz, T.M., T. Steelman, J. Carmin, K. Korfmacher and C. Moseley (2004). *Collaborative environmental management: What roles for government?* Washington, DC: Resources for the Future Press.

Lee, K. (1993). *Compass and gyroscope: Integrating science and politics for the environment.* Washington, DC: Island Press.

Lejano, R. and H. Ingram (2008). 'How social networks enable adaptation to system complexity and extreme weather events', in C. Pahl-Wostl, P. Kabat and J. Moltgen (eds), *Adaptive and integrated water management*, pp. 249–62. Berlin Heidelberg: Springer-Verlag.

Lise, W. (2000). 'Factors influencing people's participation in forest management in India', *Ecological Economics*, 34(3): 379–92.

MA (2005). *The millennium ecosystem assessment—ecosystems and human well-being: Synthesis.* Washington DC: Island Press.

Majone, G. and Wildavsky, A. (1978). 'Implementation as evolution', *Policy Studies Review*, 12: 103–17.

Manitoba Agricultural Services Corporation (MASC) (2007a). 'Drought pasture insurance pilot program'. Retrieved March 2007 from MASC, www.masc.mb.ca/masc_ins.nsf/pasture_drought.html?OpenPage&charset=iso-8859-1.

———. (2007b). 'Fall frost insurance pilot pro-gram'. Retrieved March 2007 from MASC, www.masc.mb.ca/masc_ins.nsf/fall_frost.html?OpenPage&charset=iso-8859-1.

Manitoba Crop Insurance Commission (MCIC). (1 December 1954). Report of the Manitoba Crop Insurance Commission. The Legislature of Manitoba, Appointed by Order-in-Council.

Manitoba Crop Insurance Review Committee (MCIRC) (June 1992). Report of the Manitoba Crop Insurance Review Committee on Canada-Manitoba Crop Insurance. The Legislature of Manitoba.

Manitoba Economic Survey Board (MESB). (February 1940). *Crop insurance in Manitoba: A report on the feasibility and practicability of crop insurance in Manitoba*. Prepared by the Economic Survey Board of Manitoba.

Marchau, V.A. and W.E. Walker (2003). 'Dealing with uncertainty in implementing advanced driver assistance systems: An adaptive approach', *Integrated Assessment*, 4(1): 35–45.

Margerum, R.D. (2007). 'Overcoming locally based collaboration constraints', *Society and Natural Resources*, 20(2): 135–52.

Mayo Clinic (21–22 March 2003). *Conference on complexity science in practice: Understanding and acting to improve health and healthcare*. Rochester, Minnesota. Retrieved August 2004 from www.complexityscience.org/index.php.

McCann, K.S. (2000). 'The diversity-stability debate', *Nature*, 405: 228–33.

McKay, J. and G.B. Keremane (2006). 'Farmers' perception on self created water management rules in a pioneer scheme: The mula irrigation scheme, India', *Irrigation and Drainage Systems*, 20(2–3): 205–23.

Ministry of Finance, Canada (2006). 'News release: Review finds Canada pension plan is financially sound'. Retrieved June 2008 from Department of Finance, Canada, www.fin.gc.ca/news06/06-026e.html.

Mitchell, M. and M. MacLeod (2006). 'Is farm diversification an effective risk management strategy?' The 2006 Rural Futures Conference, University of Plymouth, UK, 5–7 April. The Rural Citizen: Governance, Culture and Well-being in the 21st century.

Mitra, S. and J.S. Sareen (2006). Adaptive policy case study: Agricultural price policy in India. In *Designing policies in a world of uncertainty, change and surprise: Adaptive policy-making for agriculture and water resources in the face of climate change*, pp. 35–68. The International Institute for Sustainable Development and The Energy and Resources Institute (eds). Retrieved June 2008 from IISD, www.iisd.org/climate/vulnerability/policy_insights.asp.

Modelski, G. (1996). 'Evolutionary paradigm for global politics', *International Studies Quarterly*, 40(3): 321–42.

Moench, M. and A. Dixit (eds) (2007). *Working with the winds of change: Towards strategies for responding to the risks associated with climate change and other hazards*. Nepal: ISET and Kathmandu, Nepal ProVention.

Moench, M., A. Dixit, S. Janakarajan, M.S. Rathore and S. Mudrakartha (2003). *The fluid mosaic: Water governance in the context of variability, uncertainty and change*. Kathmandu, Nepal: Nepal Water Conservation Foundation and Colorado, USA: Institute for Social and Enviromental Transition.

Moseley, C. (1999). 'New ideas, old institutions: Environment, community and state in the Pacific Northwest', unpublished doctoral dissertation, Yale University, New Haven, CT.

Naik, G. and A.H. Kalro (2000). 'A methodology for assessing impact of irrigation management transfer from farmers' perspective', *Water Policy*, 2: 445–60.

Nair, S. (2009). *Understanding adaptive policy mechanisms through power subsidies for agriculture in Andhra Pradesh, India*. The Energy and Resources Institute. Retrieved from http://www.iisd. org/climate/vulnerability/policy_communities.asp.

National Round Table on the Environment and the Economy (NRTEE) (2007). 'Getting to 2050: Canada's transition to a low-emission future'. Report of the National Round Table on the Environment and the Economy. Government of Canada. Retrieved July 2008 from NRTEE, http://www.trnee-nrtee.gc.ca/eng/publications/getting-to-2050/index-getting-to-2050.php.

Nichol, L. (2005). *Irrigation water markets in southern Alberta*. MA Thesis, Department of Economics, University of Lethbridge. Lethbridge, Alberta.

O'Hara, P. (2006). 'Shaping the key to fit the lock: Participatory action research and community forestry in the Philippines', in S. Tyler (ed.), *Communities, livelihoods and natural resources: Action research and policy change in Asia*, pp. 253–73. Ottawa: ITDG and IDRC.

O'Toole, K. and N. Burdess (2004). 'New community governance in small rural towns: The Australian experience', *Journal of Rural Studies*, 20(4): 433–43.

Oxford University Press. (n.d.). Retrieved 3 May 2008 from European Union Politics Glossary, http://www.oup.com/uk/orc/bin/9780199281954/01student/flashcards/glossary.htm#S. Oxford: Oxford University Press.

Pahl-Wostl, C. (2008). *Adaptive and integrated water management: Coping with complexity and uncertainty*. Berlin Heidelberg: Springer.

Perri. (1997). *Escaping poverty: From safety nets to networks of opportunity*. London: Demos.

Policy Research Initiative (PRI) (2005). *Social capital as a public policy tool: Project report*. Retrieved June 2008 from Government of Canada, www.policyresearch.gc.ca/doclib/PR_SC_SocialPolicy_200509_e.pdf.

PRAYAS (2004). *India Power Reforms Update*. Issue no. 9.

Producer Payment Panel (1994). *Implications of changing the western grain transportation act payment*. Technical report of the producer payment panel, March, E.W. Tyrchniewicz (Chairman). Available at the Manitoba Legislative Library, Canada.

Putnam, R. (2001). 'Social capital: Measurement and consequences', *ISUMA—Canadian Journal of Policy Research*, 2(1): 41–55.

Ralston, B. and I. Wilson (2006). *The scenario planning handbook: Developing strategies in uncertain times*. United States: Thompson-Southwestern.

RAND Europe (1997). 'Complex systems theory and development practice: Understanding non-linear realities'. Retrieved July 2008 from http://rand.org/pubs/drafts/2007/DRU1514.pdf.

Ribot, J. (2004). *Waiting for democracy: The politics of choice in natural resource decentralization*. Washington, DC: World Resources Institute.

Rigaux, L.R. and R.H. Singh (1977). *Benefit-cost evaluation of improved levels of agricultural drainage in Manitoba*, Volume 1, Volume 2. Research Bulletin No. 77-1. Department of Agricultural Economics and Farm Management, University of Manitoba, Canada.

Rihani, S. (2002). *Complex systems theory and development practice: Understanding non-linear realities*. New York: Zed Books.

Ritchey, T. (2005). *Futures studies using morphological analysis*. Adapted from an article for the UN University Millennium Project. Retrieved 11 September 2008 from the Swedish Morphological Society, www.swemorph.com.

Rittel, H.W.J. and M.M. Webber (1973). 'Dilemmas in a general theory of planning', *Policy Sciences*, 4(2): 155–69.

Roberts, N. (1997). 'Public deliberation: An alternative approach to crafting policy and setting direction', *Public Administration Review*, 57(2): 124–32.

———. (2004). 'Public deliberation in an age of direct citizen participation', *American Review of Public Administration*, 34(4): 315–53.

Rondinelli, D.A. (1981). 'Government decentralization in comparative perspective: Developing countries', *International Review of Administrative Science*, 47(2): 133–45.

———. (1993). *Development projects as policy experiments: An adaptive approach to development administration*. 2nd edition. New York: Routledge.

Rothman, D. (2007). Personal communication with Dale S. Rothman, senior researcher, International Institute for Sustainable Development.

Rotmans, J. (1998). 'Methods for IA: The challenges and opportunities ahead', *Environmental Modeling and Assessment*, 3(3): 155–79.

Roy, D., H. Venema and D. Swanson (2007). *Understanding adaptive policy mechanisms through farm-level studies of adaptation to weather events in Saskatchewan, Canada*. International Institute for Sustainable Development. Retrieved from www.iisd.org/climate/vulnerability/policy_communities.asp.

Ruitenbeek, J. and C. Cartier (2001). *The invisible wand: Adaptive co-management as an emergent strategy in complex bio-economic systems*. Occasional paper No. 34. Bogor Barat, Indonesia: Centre for International Forestry Research.

Rush, R., J. Ivey, R. de Loe and R. Kreitzwiser (2004). 'Adapting to climate change in the Oldman River Watershed, Alberta: A discussion paper for watershed stakeholders', Discussion Paper produced by the Guelph Water Management Group, University of Guelph, Guelph, Ontario.

Ryfe, D.M. (2005). 'Does deliberative democracy work?' *Annual Review of Political Science*, 8: 49–71.

Sabatier, P. and H. Jenkins-Smith (1999). 'The advocacy coalition framework: An assessment', in P. Sabatier (ed.), pp. 117–68. *Theories of the policy process*. Boulder, Colorado: Westview Press.

Sachs, J.D. (2008). *Common wealth: Economics for a crowded planet*. New York: The Penguin Press.

Sathirathai, S. (1998). *Economic valuation of mangroves and the roles of local communities in the conservation of natural resources: Case study of Surat Thani, south of Thailand*. Bangkok: Centre for Ecological Economics, Chulalongkorn University; Singapore: Economy and Environment Program for Southeast Asia (EEPSEA).

Schwartz, P. (1991). *The art of the long view: Planning for the future in an uncertain world*. New York: Currency Doubleday.

Scoones, I. (2004). 'Climate change and the challenge of non-equilibrium thinking', *IDS Bulletin*, 35(3): 114–19.

Senge, P. (1990). *The fifth discipline: The art and practice of the learning organization*. New York: Currency Doubleday.

Smith, P. (1998). 'The use of subsidies for soil and water conservation: A case study from western India', Agricultural Research and Extension Network Paper 87. Overseas Development Institute, London.

Steinemann, A. and B. Norton (2003). 'Environmental values and adaptive management', in B. Norton (ed.), *Searching for sustainability: Interdisciplinary essays in philosophy of conservation biology*, pp. 514–48. Cambridge, UK: Cambridge University Press.

Stone, D. (2001). Learning lessons, policy transfer and the international diffusion of policy ideas. CSGR Working Paper No. 69/01. Coventry, UK, Centre for the Study of Globalisation and Regionalisation: 40.

Swanson, D. and H.D. Venema (2006). 'Adaptive policy case study: Analysis of the crow rate in Prairie Canada: A cautionary tale', in *Designing policies in a world of uncertainty, change and surprise: Adaptive policy-making for agriculture and water resources in the face of climate Change*, pp. 97–116. The International Institute for Sustainable Development and The Energy and Resources Institute (eds). Retrieved June 2008 from www.iisd.org/climate/vulnerability/policy_communities.asp.

——— (2007). 'Understanding adaptive policy mechanisms through farm-level studies of adaptation to weather events in Manitoba, Canada'. Retrieved September 2008 from www.iisd.org/climate/vulnerability/policy_communities.asp.

Swanson, D., H.D. Venema, C. Rust, J. Medlock and A. McCoy (2008). *Understanding adaptive policy mechanisms through farm-level studies of adaptation to weather events in Alberta, Canada*. International Institute for Sustainalble Development. Retrieved from www.iisd.org/climate/vulnerability/policy_communities.asp.

Tomar, S. and S. Nair (2008). *Adaptive policies community case study: Participatory watershed management in Maharashtra, India*. The Energy and Resources Institute. Retrieved from www.iisd.org/climate/vulnerability/policy_communities.asp.

——— (2009). *Understanding adaptive policy mechanisms through farm-level cast study of weather-related shocks and stresses in Meghalaya, India*. The Energy and Resources Institute. Retrieved from http://www.iisd.org/climate/vulnerability/policy_communities.asp.

Tyler, S. (2006). *Natural resource co-management: Local learning for poverty reduction*. Ottawa: IDRC.

UK Cabinet Office (2003). *Trying it out: The role of 'pilots' in policy-making* (*Report of a review of government pilot*). UK: Government Chief Social Researcher's Office, Cabinet Office.

UNEP. (2000). *The ecosystem approach: Decision taken at the Fifth Conference of the Parties to the Convention on Biological Diversity*. United Nations Environment Programme. Retrieved July 2008 from Convention on Biological Diversity, www.cbd.int/decisions/?m=COP-05&id=7148&lg=0.

Van Kemenade, S., S. Paradis and É. Jenkins (2003). 'Can public policy address social capital?' *Horizons: Policy Research Initiative*, 6(1): 31–34.

Walker, B. and D. Salt (2006). *Resilience thinking: Sustaining ecosystems and people in a changing world*. Washington, DC: Island Press.

Walker, B., S. Carpenter, J. Anderies, N. Abel, G. Cumming, M. Janssen et al. (2002). 'Resilience management in social-ecological systems: A working hypothesis for a participatory approach', *Conservation Ecology*, 6(1): 14. Retrieved September 2008 from www.consecol.org/vol6/iss1/art14.

Walker, W.E., S.A. Rahman and J. Cave (2001). 'Adaptive policies, policy analysis, and policy-making', *European Journal of Operational Research*, 128(2): 282–89.

Walker, W.E. and V.A.W. J. Marchau (2003). 'Dealing with uncertainty in policy analysis and policy-making', *Integrated Assessment*, 4(1): 1–4.

Wallington, T.J. and G. Lawrence (2007). 'Making democracy matter: Responsibility and effective environmental governance in regional Australia', *Journal of Rural Studies*, 24: 277–90.

Wheatly, M.J. (1999). *Leadership and the new science. Discovering order in a chaotic world*. 2nd edition. San Francisco: Berrett-Koehler.

About the Organizations, Editors and Contributors

THE ORGANIZATIONS

International Development Research Centre
www.idrc.ca

Canada's International Development Research Centre (IDRC) is one of the world's leading institutions in the generation and application of new knowledge to meet the challenges of international development. For nearly 40 years, IDRC has worked in close collaboration with researchers from the developing world to build healthier, more equitable and more prosperous societies.

International Institute for Sustainable Development
www.iisd.org

The International Institute for Sustainable Development (IISD) contributes to sus-tainable development by advancing policy recommendations on international trade and investment, economic policy, climate change, measurement and assessment, and natural resources management. Through the Internet, we report on international negotiations and share knowledge gained through collaborative projects with global partners, resulting in more rigorous research, capacity building in developing countries and better dialogue between North and South.

IISD's vision is better living for all—sustainably; its mission is to champion innovation, enabling societies to live sustainably. IISD is registered as a charitable organization in Canada and has 501(c)(3) status in the United States. IISD receives core operating support from the Government of Canada, provided through the Canadian International Development Agency (CIDA), the International Development Research Centre (IDRC) and Environment Canada and from the Province of Manitoba. The Institute receives project funding from numerous governments inside and outside Canada, United Nations agencies, foundations and the private sector.

The Energy and Resources Institute
www.teriin.org

The Energy and Resources Institute (TERI) is a not-for-profit research organization working in the fields of energy, environment and sustainable development. Founded in 1974, TERI is a unique developing-country institution with a global vision and local focus, and has been at the forefront of researching, formulating and implementing sustainable development strategies for India and the world.

THE EDITORS

Darren Swanson is a Senior Project Manager with the Measurement and Assessment Program at the International Institute for Sustainable Development (IISD) in Canada. He is a sustainable development policy specialist and professional engineer with 17 years of consulting and research experience. He works with governments at all levels and from around the world on strategic processes for organizational and societal-wide learning and adaptive management, including sustainable development strategies, indicator information systems, integrated assessment methods and adaptive policy-making approaches. He holds a Master of Public Administration degree in international development from the Kennedy School of Government at Harvard University, a Master of Geo-environmental Engineering degree from the University of Saskatchewan, Canada and a Bachelor's degree in civil engineering.

Suruchi Bhadwal is an Area Convener of the Centre for Global Environment Research at The Energy and Resources Institute (TERI) in India. She has a Master of Environmental Sciences degree. Her work focuses on community-level impacts, vulnerability and adaptation assessment. She was principal investigator of the World Bank-funded project in India on 'Addressing vulnerability to climate variability and change through assessment of adaptation issues and options'. She is a lead author contributing to the Fourth Assessment Report of the Intergovernmental Panel on Climate Change (IPCC), Working Group II.

THE CONTRIBUTORS

Stephan Barg (Steve) is an Associate and long-time Senior Corporate Advisor with the International Institute for Sustainable Development (IISD) in Canada.

He has undertaken research on many sustainable development issues, but his central interests are the connections between government and corporate policy and the tools used in each arena to foster sustainable development. This work builds on his previous experience as a government finance official and as a corporate finance and planning executive. He has a Bachelor of Science degree from McGill University and a Master of Philosophy degree (Economics of Public Finance) from England's University of York.

John Drexhage is Director of the Climate Change and Energy Program at the International Institute for Sustainable Development (IISD) in Canada. His work on climate change is based on 15 years of experience on the issue, first as a domestic advisor and international negotiator with the government of Canada, and then as an expert analyst for IISD. His expertise covers a broad range of areas related to climate change, and he is currently focusing on regulatory frameworks for greenhouse gas emissions, post-2012 climate change regimes, market-based instruments and more fully exploring linkages between adaptation, mitigation and sustainable development. He is a lead author with Working Group III of the Intergovernmental Panel on Climate Change.

Sreeja Nair is a Research Associate with the Climate Change Division at The Energy and Resources Institute (TERI) in India. Her work focuses on climate change impacts, vulnerability and adaptation assessment and policy analysis. She is an inter-disciplinary researcher with a Bachelor of Biomedical Sciences degree and a Masters of Environmental Studies degree. She works on cross-cutting issues and policy analysis related to climate change, across natural and social sciences. Her work explores the social dimensions of synergies and conflicts among population, environment and development.

Dimple Roy is a Manager with the Sustainable Natural Resources Management Program at the International Institute for Sustainable Development (IISD) in Canada. She holds a Master of Environmental Design degree from the University of Calgary and a Bachelor of Architecture degree. Her training and experience include a variety of roles in environmental education, policy research and analysis, and project management in non-governmental organizations and government agencies. Her current policy research is in integrated water resources management, watershed governance and market-based instruments for resource management. Prior to joining IISD, Dimple worked with the Manitoba provincial government in Canada, conducting policy and legislative analysis and coordinating the Manitoba Round Table for Sustainable Development, a multi-stakeholder group comprising eight provincial ministers and members of the public representing various interests in sustainable development.

Sanjay Tomar is a Natural Resource Management and Climate Change Adaptation Specialist with 10 years of research and professional experience. He is a Fellow with the Climate Change Division at The Energy and Resources Institute (TERI) in India. He holds a PhD in Forestry with specialization in Landscape Ecology from the Indian Institute of Remote Sensing, Department of Space, Dehradun, India. His work focuses on policy analysis, impact and vulnerability assessment, and implementation of projects addressing climate change adaptation to increase the resilience of communities. He has extensive experience in capacity building and training for watershed management and agriculture extension management. Prior to joining TERI, he worked with the German Agency for Technical Cooperation (GTZ) for implementing the Indo-German Bilateral Project on Capacity Building and Training.

Stephen Tyler is President of Adaptive Resource Management Ltd., an interdisciplinary consulting practice in Victoria, British Columbia specializing in community-oriented natural resource management and adaptation studies. Recent work includes climate adaptation studies in Asia and Canada; design of adaptive resource management frameworks; as well as planning and evaluating capacity development to implement innovative resource management frameworks. From 1997 to 2005, he was team leader for the Community-based Natural Resource Management Program of the International Development Research Centre (IDRC). The programme he led at IDRC engaged researchers from a dozen Asian countries in developing and testing innovative resource management strategies, now being implemented in many countries through reforms to national policies and local governance. He has worked as a policy analyst, consultant and researcher on environment, energy and development issues with governments, research institutions and international agencies in Canada, the US and Asia. He holds a PhD in City and Regional Planning from the University of California, Berkeley.

Henry David Venema (Hank) is Director of the Sustainable Natural Resources Management Program at the International Institute for Sustainable Development (IISD) in Canada. He is a professional engineer and natural resource management consultant with extensive experience in rural development, environmental economics, water resources planning and energy sector planning in North America, Africa and Asia. He holds a Master of Water Resources Engineering degree from the University of Ottawa and a PhD in Systems Design Engineering from the University of Waterloo. Dr Venema leads IISD's current research on the valuation of natural capital in Prairie Canada; institutional linkages between payments for ecosystem services and integrated water resources management in prairie watersheds and governance models for Lake Winnipeg stewardship.

Index